EYEWITNESS TO HISTORY
A PERSONAL JOURNAL

By ROBERT SCHRAGE

Eyewitness to History: A Personal Journal

ISBN: 978-0-9887117-2-3

Author: Robert Schrage

Cover artwork by: Kevin T. Kelly
Front cover photo by: Jymi Bolden

Published by:

The Merlot Group, LLC: 226 W Pike St-Suite One, Covington KY 41011 (859) 743-1003, www.merlotgroup.com

The merlotgroup
MARKETING + DESIGN

To Ann, my wife and soul mate. Thanks for all the support as I went on these adventures. You're the best!

FOREWARD

Bob Schrage and I have been great friends for over 20 years. Early in our friendship we realized we shared a common love of history, government, and travel. That realization started us on a series of trips to historic events that have enriched our lives and deepened our friendship. These ranged from well planned, always by Bob, to spur of the moment. Bob is a planner and collector, who conscientiously maintains a journal of all his travels. I, on the other hand, don't collect, don't journal, and don't enjoy planning trips. I've always known that I had the best part of the deal. However, I am good at seizing the moment and on a number of occasions was able to get us right to the center of the action.

One of those times was when Bob and I decided to go to Frankfort, KY to watch the inauguration parade for Governor Paul Patton, a democrat. The weather was clear but cold and the parade was long, winding its way to the capitol building. We decided to get out of the cold for a while and went into a small pub at the foot of the avenue leading to the Capitol. We had a beer and watched the parade on a television over the bar. Once we were warmed up, we headed back out to the parade itself. A short way up the hill we saw a green trolley car serving as a float in the parade and carrying members of the Oldham County Democratic Party. On the spur of the moment I said, "let's go", and headed for the float. Bob hadn't heard me and looked up to see me running to catch up with the float, at which point he started running after me. We jumped onto the rear step of the moving float and stepped inside the trolley. The people inside were surprised to see us and I said "Hi, we're from Northern Kentucky." One of the fellows said "Oh, a couple of republicans, huh?" because our part of the state was so predominantly republican. We both laughed and said "yes". He laughingly replied, "Well, that's ok, we're friendly in Oldham County. Welcome aboard!" A few minutes later the parade halted for a brief stop – right in front of the viewing stand where Governor Patton was watching the parade and waving to everyone. We were about five feet away directly in front of the Governor and so we waved to him, too. We called out "Congratulations!", and he smiled and said "Thanks". Then the float began to continue on.

We got off at the Capitol and said, "Well, that was fun – a couple of Northern Kentucky Republicans waving and congratulating the Governor from right directly in front of him." It was a perfect addition to our quirky traveling experiences.

On another occasion during the 2000 Presidential primary campaign, Bob and I went to Iowa for the Caucuses. We were a few feet away from George W. Bush at his first election night victory party. A less notable but unusual example of being in the right place at the right time involved Senator Orrin Hatch, Senior Senator from Utah, who had been campaigning for President during the primary. We had heard that there would be an event the following afternoon at the Iowa Caucus Media Center, located in an arena. We were sure that Hatch would be announcing that he was dropping out of the race. This was a press-only event with restricted entry. Obviously, we had to act like reporters and sneak into the event. The key to getting into places you're not supposed to be is to act completely confident and walk right in with no hesitation. Bob and I had mastered this skill through many repetitions. We entered and first stopped by the food table. Reporters must like to eat because we have always found and enjoyed a good spread in the press area of these events. After that, Bob said, "I'm sure the Senator will enter through that door on the upper level and go down those steps in the central aisle on his way to the dais." So we staked out a spot at the foot of the stairs. Sure enough, that's how Senator Hatch entered. Because of our position, we were both able shake his hand and express encouragement concerning his campaign even though we were sure he was dropping out. He is a distinguished and professional looking man as are all senators. They're part of one of the most elite groups in the world as one of only 100 people who hold that office out of hundreds of millions of people in the country.

As he walked toward the platform where he would make his announcement, the press – reporters and cameramen – swarmed around him calling out questions and stretching out microphones and cameras to capture his answers. The crowd was so thick that he stopped in the middle of the gym floor and proceeded to answer questions, but he was not dropping out. He did, however, drop out the next day after a last place finish. Bob and I thought, "What the heck, we might as well join in the press conference." I kept moving us around the crowd until we were immediately behind and to either side of the Senator looking over his shoulders about one to two feet behind him. I was the city administrator of Erlanger KY, at the time, and was wearing a City of Erlanger sweat shirt underneath an open black bomber jacket. We left the gym feeling that we had accomplished our goals – we made it into the site, enjoyed a free snack, shook hands with the presidential candidate and were right in the middle of the action during his press conference. It had been a good day in which we achieved our purpose for these historic trips, which is to experience the on-the-ground, real life context of events that will be recorded in history books, but won't include the contextual details that we experience.

The best part, though, was that when we returned home and were walking through the airport, we heard something on the television monitors that sounded familiar. We looked up and lo and behold there were Bill and Bob on national television right behind the Senator as he answered questions about his campaign. Even better, there was my City of Erlanger sweatshirt for all the world, or at least early morning CNN viewers, to see.

As Bob mentions in the book, we both feel that protesters serve a worthwhile function. They are living proof that all citizens of the United States of America have a right to peacefully express their opinions and advocate their positions in public. Most protestors are peaceful and fairly orderly. Sometimes, though, they are unruly and obnoxious. Even so, they have a right to protest, but not to infringe on other people's rights to peaceful and unobstructed use of the public rights of way. We came across a perfect example of this latter type of protest as we were walking along the street during one of Bill Clinton's inaugurations when gay rights and "don't ask, don't tell" were hot issues. In this case, a group of young people were protesting against gay rights and were being led by an adult of dubious intelligence and no taste. The signs they were waving depicted crude drawings of males engaging in sex acts with the written message, "God Hates Gays". The young people were being exhorted by their adult leader to make loud derogatory statements about the moral shortcomings of gay people and tell one and all passersby that "God really did hate gay people because they were an abomination."

Bob and I normally observe protests, but don't get involved and that was our intention in this case. Bob was successful in executing that strategy. I, on the other hand, started out ok, but quickly reached a point where I couldn't stand by and let this idiotic, clearly uneducated, and behaviorally bankrupt "adult" teach these young people to behave in such a judgmental and hurtful, not to mention STUPID way. So, I very calmly said, "Excuse me buddy......why are you teaching these young people to act this way?" He didn't respond calmly. He got in my face and said, "Because God hates gays!!!!" I felt compelled to respond by saying, "I talk to God every day and He's never once told me He hates gays. In fact, since we're all His children and He loves us all then you obviously don't know what you're talking about!" With that, we were off to the races. After a few minutes of listening to his lame brained and insulting statements my voice got louder and louder, and I heard Bob saying "Come on, Bill, let's get out of here." I concluded our discussion by saying, "You're an idiot!" We then walked on our way to experience more of the Inauguration sights and sounds. Sometimes there's nothing like being part of the action.

Every year during the Christmas and New Year holiday season, Bob and I go to Spring Grove Cemetery in Cincinnati OH and visit the gravesite of Salmon P. Chase, who has a connection to Cincinnati, and also to Northern Kentucky in that Chase Law School at Northern Kentucky University is named after him. We recap the year just ended, discuss our various experiences, and plan for the year ahead. As you can probably tell, I cherish my friendship with Bob and truly enjoy the experiences we share. Even though I was on many of the trips Bob describes in this book, I found that I also really enjoyed reading his descriptions and hearing his perspective on these events.

I'll close by recounting two related experiences. Just this past weekend, I was watching a television documentary about John Wilkes Booth and the events surrounding the assassination of

Abraham Lincoln. During the show, I saw two places that Bob and I had visited and had found ways to make our experiences more than just those of normal tourists.

The first was Ford's Theater. We had both been there on other occasions, both individually and together. On one of our many trips to Washington D.C., we went to the theater, but wanted to experience a deeper connection. We considered the modern arrangement of the streets around the theater and figured out a path that ended at the back door of the theater. This was where Booth had handed over the reins of his horse to a stagehand to hold while he entered the theater to kill Lincoln. The back of the theater lies at the end of an alley. The bricks of the walls and the wooden door with iron fittings are still the original ones that were there on the night of the assassination. We like to physically touch old surfaces in order to form a physical and psychic bond with the past events that took place in these locations. In this case, we each touched the walls and door, and took time to envision the moments in 1865 during which the tragic events occurred. We also stood facing out of the alley and pictured Booth with his flowing cape and broken ankle riding his horse out of the alley and into history. As I watched the documentary, it showed the alley, walls and door and described the events I've just related. There was a re-enactment of Booth galloping off into the night. I thought of that trip, our friendship and the many life experiences we've shared with one another.

On a different trip, in this case to Barack Obama's first inauguration, Bob and his son, Ethan, and I and my son, John, were in Chinatown trying to decide on a place to have lunch. We found ourselves on H Street in front of a Chinese restaurant. Since we all like Chinese food, we decided to eat there. However, before entering I noticed an historic informational sign next to the building. We were amazed to realize that this building was Mary Surratt's Washington boarding house where the conspirators in the assassination plot often met to discuss their political grievances and plan the assassination. Mary Surratt was the first woman ever hanged in the United States. The building still looks the same as it did in 1865 and in all the historic photos. The only difference is that a set of wooden steps leading up to a small second story porch have been removed and the first floor has been converted to the Wok-n-Roll Chinese and Japanese Restaurant. We had an excellent lunch in which the boys sat at a counter and ate sushi for the first time, while Bob and I had other Asian dishes. A fine time was had by all eating Chinese and Japanese food in the very building where the Lincoln conspirators had plotted President Lincoln's assassination over 145 years before. It was a great Bob and Bill experience made even more special because we shared it with our sons. Now a few years later I could re-experience this unexpected and unique event as the building was shown as part of the documentary and I thought of the many interesting and rewarding experiences I've enjoyed because of this special friendship. I hope that in reading this book, you will feel that you too are a part of these adventures.

Bill Scheyer
February 26, 2013

Bill Scheyer and Bob: An annual visit to the grave of Salmon P. Chase

INTRODUCTION

It was on a cold, rainy day in June of 1973 that my father really turned me on to the idea of going to historic events as they happen. It was perhaps the best time of my childhood. Following his retirement from the United States Post Office, we started taking annual vacations. In 1973, we found ourselves in Canada at Niagara Falls. Queen Elizabeth II was in the country with her husband, Prince Phillip. We followed the visit through the papers and Dad read the Queen was going to be in St. Catherine's near Toronto. He said, "Let's go see the Queen." So, early one morning we took off on our quest to see the monarch of England and her husband. We arrived in St. Catherine's quite early and sat in a park talking with some people from the community. They were specifically interested in Dad's impression of the Watergate mess and what would happen to President Nixon. Dad had few kind words for the President and felt he needed to resign.

The streets were lined with people although the rain fell most of the morning. Eventually, anticipation built and in the short distance a car approached with the Queen and the Prince waving as it drove by directly in front of a father and son from Kentucky. It was over in a couple minutes

The bug bit me and I was now hooked on not only reading about history, but seeing it.

Gerald Ford dedicated the Environmental Protection Agency Building in Cincinnati. This started a string of Presidential handshakes that continues with every president through Obama. When 1976 came around and America was deciding whom to elect between President Ford and Jimmy Carter, it was necessary to attend candidate appearances and follow the campaign closely. I was sixteen. In the fall of 1976, Dad was in the hospital with appendicitis, but Jimmy Carter was at Lunken Airport in Cincinnati. I shook his hand twice and then went to visit Dad in the hospital. The year 1976 was the bicentennial year of our country and Dad took me to every event he could. In 1980, things were taken to an all new level. I was so inspired by Ronald Reagan, but went to Carter and John Anderson events as well. Anderson, the Congressman from Illinois, ran a respectable third party campaign and on election night I went to his headquarters in downtown Cincinnati. The workers were generally happy with his showing, but not happy a couple Reagan supporters stopped by. One of Reagan's last big campaign stops was the Sunday before the election in Cincinnati and included President Ford and Bob Hope. Thirty Equal Rights Amendment supporters protested aggressively before the doors were opened to the Convention Center. Dad and I were there enjoying every minute.

Now in my early fifties I have a lifetime of stories and memories of much more than just campaign appearances. Many of the events attended defined America in the last forty years including the Impeachment of the President of the United States, the execution of a most evil man, the funeral of an icon, the most controversial election in history, the long overdue celebration and recognition of the Greatest Generation, inaugurations including that of the first African American President, and election history too strange to believe.

The stories told in this book are just a handful I could have selected. Some are funny, some sad, some inspiring, and others hard to define. My father taught me a love of Country and took me places; I have tried to pass this down to my children. My son, Andrew, who died in an accident while away at college in 2011, will never go on other trips. On the night, he died we were scheduled to leave for Florida to watch the last launch of the Space Shuttle. He told his boss he was mostly looking forward to just talking with his Dad on the long trip. Thinking of this special comment, tears fall on my writing paper.

As parents, it is most important to spend time with your children. Not everyone is going to go to historical events like this, but whether you do or not, write down the stories you do experience.

Otherwise they will be lost. History exists in the everyday occurrences in the life of parents and children. Document them!

Let me admit right up front to being a moderate republican with serious problems with both political parties. History is to be loved whether it is republican or democratic history; good or bad. It would have been great to be at Ford's Theater in April of 1865 or at VE Day on Times Square in 1945. It's all history to me. There are no regrets, only great memories. As Harry Truman said when asked about history; "it's one damn thing after another." I have a mind full of great stories to share, but more importantly I was there when things happened. When reading about historical events, I always wonder what it was like to be there. My stories in some small way will, hopefully, tell others what it was like at the events of our time. In addition, it is my goal that they be as interesting to read about as they were to witness.

Robert Schrage
Rabbit Hash, KY
2013

CHAPTER ONE

REAGAN'S ACCEPTANCE SPEECH

One of my favorite memories of an historic event was the 1980 Republican National Convention held in Detroit, Michigan. As a youth delegate, I was selected several times to be on the floor of the convention and was there as Ronald Reagan secured enough delegates to officially become the nominee of the Republican Party. Balloons fell and the crowd celebrated as the long primary campaign officially ended. Reagan was now the nominee and as the crowd demonstrated for a long time, a twenty year old college student from Ludlow, Kentucky was in awe of what was being witnessed.

Twenty years later, I was also on the floor in 2000 as George Bush went over the top in delegates and officially became the nominee of the Republican Party. However, it was nothing like 1980.

The night after Reagan went over the top in delegates, found me again on the convention floor. I supported George Bush in the primary but in hindsight it was a wrong choice. However, I did have a job on the Bush campaign during the Wisconsin primary. My role was advance work for Bush as he ran against Governor Reagan. It included going to campaign stops ahead of the candidate, and often staying for the events. I met Bush many times and experienced a lot of events and press conferences. Bush was a very nice person. As a result, my choice was to support Bush for the Vice Presidency at the 1980 convention. I thought the ticket needed balance between a conservative and a moderate. This convention, unlike today, had the suspense of not announcing the Vice President ahead of time. Reagan had not decided. He even considered former President Ford for the Vice Presidency, but Ford wanted certain powers in what would have amounted to a co-presidency and was dropped from consideration.

I wore my Bush for Vice President buttons and carried signs in support. Less than twenty-four hours before the nomination speech, Bush was announced as Reagan's choice. I was ecstatic. In my mind this was the last great convention, for it had suspense and excitement.

On the last night of the convention, as Reagan started his historic first ever acceptance speech, I was eight feet in front of him on the floor. "With a deep awareness of the responsibility conferred by your trust, I accept your nomination for the Presidency of the United States." Thus began the fall campaign that would throw Carter out of office and elect one of the greatest presidents we have ever had. Reagan said, "More than anything else, I want my candidacy to unify our country; to renew the American spirit and sense of purpose. I want to carry our message to every American, regardless of party affiliation, who is a member of this community of shared values." I screamed in approval, touched by this man inspiring me to be a better citizen—a better American. I had a chill from the excitement and felt the moment like no other in my life. This was true history. Reagan would bring a new direction to this country and it started right there.

I felt I could reach out and touch Reagan as he hovered above me just a few feet away. Not like you would a rock star or as a fan toward a favorite entertainer. That is too much like an idol. As a twenty year old college student I was so inspired about his hope and positive attitude about America. "The time is now, my fellow Americans, to recapture our destiny, to take it into our own hands." I cheered as loud as possible. As I felt I could reach out and touch him; I imagine so did the person in the last row of Joe Lewis Arena that night. His words were so awe inspiring. I became a solid Reagan fan and worked hard in the fall for his election. He inspired me that summer night in a way no public official has since. Of all the historic events I have attended this is probably my favorite. Maybe because I was young and it was such a special memory that week in Detroit. When you are young and a little lost you look or need some inspiration. Whether I was looking for it or it presented itself, I found inspiration that night.

The impact of Reagan still lives with me. Today, I wish there was a Reagan to get through all the political partisanship. The far right likes to claim Reagan but they are far from Reagan like.

His style of making you feel good, strong leadership, honesty and bi-partisanship is missing. The left never liked him and today's right can't claim him.

A few months after being sworn in as President, I cried all afternoon when it was announced he was shot leaving a Washington hotel. I thought my heart had been ripped out and for the first time completely understood what my Dad's generation felt when Kennedy was assassinated.

Years later, after Reagan left office, he had brain surgery. Not long after the surgery, I met Reagan at the Cincinnatian Hotel in Cincinnati, Ohio. As my wife held our infant son, Andrew, in her arms, Reagan grabbed his tiny foot and shook it like a hand. "Hello young man," he said.

Reagan and I shook hands. However, as a father, I was most awed by the foot shake!

CHAPTER TWO

THE EXECUTION OF TIMOTHY McVEIGH

Prior to the September 11, 2001 attacks on New York City, the Oklahoma City bombing was the largest terrorist attack in American history. On April 19, 1995, 168 people were killed when Timothy McVeigh parked a truck bomb in front of a federal building and walked away. Minutes later the explosion not only ripped through the lives of thousands of people, but also the heart of America. The aspect of the event standing out to me the most was the image of Timothy McVeigh walking past the first floor day care center and all the innocent children. Nineteen children were killed. In the book, "American Terrorist: Timothy McVeigh and the Oklahoma City Bombing," he calls the children killed "collateral damage," regretting only that their deaths detracted from his bid to avenge Waco and Ruby Ridge. I remember that sick feeling in my stomach when learning this attack was done by an American for political purposes.

Ninety minutes after the bombing that tore apart the Alfred P. Murrah Federal Building and the lives of so many, McVeigh was arrested for driving without a license plate.

The week before, my son Andrew had turned six and I can remember worrying about our country and his future. Little did I know how the story would come around and make me think about so many issues.

In the early morning of Sunday, June 10, 2001, I had breakfast with my sister during a very rare visit. My mood became somber. As the day progressed, I was dominated by the sadness of the story I was about to see concluded. On Monday morning Timothy McVeigh would be executed for the bombing in Oklahoma City.

After having dinner at a Wendy's with family, my friend Bill Scheyer and I left for Terre Haute, arriving shortly after 10 p.m. and immediately headed to Voorhees Park. At the park were seven pro-death penalty demonstrators. One who seemed to be the leader was a child psychology major at Indiana State

University. He, as well as his fellow demonstrators, was very articulate and adamant about their position. One girl said, "It's all about Timothy McVeigh here. What about the 168 people he killed? It's not about Timothy McVeigh; it's about the 168 lives. They didn't ask for a final meal, no phone calls. Why do we give him the opportunity?" The student leader told a Swedish reporter, "This is not about revenge; McVeigh didn't affect us. He didn't affect the government. He affected the 168 killed. It's about justice." This was a profound thought to me: revenge or justice? Revenge was evil; justice the American way. The words seemed good but the signs told a different story. "Remember the victims!" "Bye Bye baby killer!" "For every action there is a reaction-Timothy McVeigh die!" "Thou shall not kill 168 and live!" They seemed like nice passionate kids. Their passion seemed to be justice.

After leaving Voorhees Park, we drove up Route 63 toward the federal prison. It was dark. However, the prison with its massive size and large lights could be seen from the road. Across the street people were renting their lawn for $10 a spot and running a food stand selling drinks, corn dogs, and other items. This was an intriguing display of the American free enterprise system at an execution. Get your hotdogs here! A lady named Jan was running the food stand. She was opposed to the death penalty but said, "All the people around here think he should fry." "Most of the people in Terre Haute are in favor of the death penalty," she said. I asked her if people here were in favor of the prison being built. "Definitely! It provided a lot of jobs. Jobs the community needs." I had a soft drink and talked some more. Jan's family and friends were sitting in lawn chairs in the front yard. At least one man had a set of binoculars to look at the prison. It was 11:30 p.m. and we headed to Fairbanks Park on the River Wabash.

I pulled into the park and walked down to the shelter house where demonstrators against the death penalty were getting organized. Picnic tables were full of tee shirts, flyers, and petitions. One table had a large canvas and people could dip their hands in paint and put them on the sign. It said "Not in our names." The most interesting sign read "Why do we kill people to show that killing

people is wrong." The crowd here was much larger than the pro
death penalty advocates we visited earlier. At 12:30 a.m.,
execution day, in the park amphitheater, a presentation was held
by a man named Doug Sloan whose son was brutally murdered. I
wondered what McVeigh was doing. Did he go to sleep tonight
or is he staying up all night? I had no idea of the profound affect
the presentation would have on me even thinking about it eleven
years later.

The crowd of fifty people listened attentively as Sloan spoke.

> "A little after midnight, in the very early morning hours
> of January 22, 1997, Frank Dennis, Curtis Holsinger and
> Curtis' girlfriend arrived at the west side of Indianapolis
> and knocked on the door of the trailer where my son,
> Chad Sloan, was living. Frank and Curtis had been
> drinking heavily and smoking marijuana. When Frank
> realized that Chad was not going to give them any money,
> he pulled a gun. Chad's hands were bound and he was
> taken to a back bedroom. According to court testimony,
> Chad suffered 26 knife slashes and stab wounds over the
> entire length of his body. This included 7 stab wounds to
> the heart, 4 from the front and 3 from the back. Chad did
> not die quickly, quietly, or easily. Frank Dennis and
> Curtis Holsinger exited the bedroom in soaked clothes.
>
> I oppose the death penalty. Would I be speaking today
> were it not for the murder of Chad? Where could I go and
> who would listen if I could not say that my son was
> murdered? His death opens doors and I must walk
> through them. His death validates my right to oppose the
> death penalty. Without his death, all I would ever hear is
> "If it happened to you, you would feel different." It has
> happened to me and I do not feel different – the death
> penalty is wrong.
>
> To every proponent, every legislator, every police officer
> and prosecuting attorney and judge; to every person who
> says the death penalty is for those left behind – the
> families, the survivors – that the death penalty is to give
> us justice and closure: the execution of the murderers of

> Chad Sloan would give me nothing. To those who would
> give an execution – almost as a gift – to me, I refuse it, I
> reject it, I renounce it. For me and the hundreds of others
> like me, execution in the name of the families and
> survivors is an anathema. We are not a rationale for
> death. Such an assumption is not true and, therefore, is
> invalid as an argument for the death penalty. To those
> who would persist in proclaiming that an execution is in
> our name or for our benefit – that proclamation is a lie"

I found these words to be very powerful as I sat there and
listened. He went on to say.

> "The death penalty is wrong. We have moved from public
> execution by hanging and firing squad to private
> executions by electrocution and gas and now to lethal
> injection. Why remove it from the public view? Why
> change the method of execution to make it more humane,
> less painful, less brutal – unless there is an inherent wrong
> with the death penalty."

In closing, Sloan said,

> "Strangely enough, a successful rehabilitation means that
> the criminal personality has died and in its place is
> resurrected a person who can contribute regardless of a
> confining location. There is justice in a failed
> rehabilitation. A failed rehabilitation means that we are
> better people for the effort. A failed rehabilitation means
> that we have better protected the rights of the innocent by
> protecting the rights of the guilty, that we have chosen
> rehabilitation and life over death."

I could only sit there and take in the powerful words. I was struck
by Sloan's inherent goodness and his ability to take such a
position in light of such evil. Was I wrong in supporting the death
penalty? I couldn't help but think Sloan was a much better
person than I was. Following his remarks, I introduced myself
and shook his hand. He told me he made his remarks more
secular and he has a speech more based upon faith. The execution
is very emotional to him and he was still in the healing process.
This man seemed so remarkable to me and I wondered how I

would react in the same situation. Sloan said, "Forgiveness itself is a process-a process of transformation because forgiveness is not something you do, forgiveness is something you become. The summit of the steep hill of forgiveness can be reached only with the face-to-face declaration, I forgive you. The death penalty prevents us from being able to reach that goal. Execute Timothy McVeigh and Bud Walsh, who lost his daughter at Oklahoma City and who opposes the death penalty, will never be able to heal and grow and be able to face Timothy McVeigh and say I forgive you. That moment would not be for Timothy McVeigh, it would be for Bud Walsh. Abolishing the death penalty is not for the guilty, it is for the innocent who want to heal."

With these words on my mind, I went back to the shelter to catch a ride to the prison grounds. As I did, I thought about how hard it is to have the forgiveness Sloan talks about. It is a very spiritual idea he discusses. The spiritual path is about transcendence. This is the state where you are removed from the material world. It is a quest for self. A quest where you inspire for something higher that is not physical. All our possessions, our material world will pass away. What remains is our soul which is eternal. Sloan to have this level of forgiveness must have transcended to a higher state. I, even these years later, still enjoy the material aspects of life. Gandhi and Mother Teresa, these were people that transcended. What is important is that part of you that never passes away. Your soul! Was the story of McVeigh a sign post or a road bump in my quest? The transcendence of Sloan has raised many questions about my soul and how to get to that higher state demonstrated by his level of forgiveness. My desire for justice seemed opposite the journey to a higher state.

After going through extensive security, I found myself on a prison bus that looked straight out of the movie *The Fugitive*. It had a barred door in the front and all the windows were barred. The chairs were comfortable, being foam just like a Greyhound Bus. Two Bureau of Prisons guards stood in silence on the bus; one in the front and one in the back. There were only a few of us on the bus and we had a police escort with lights flashing. On the way to the prison, I wondered about the thoughts of prisoners sitting on this bus going for the first time to the prison, perhaps to spend the rest of their lives. Between 1:30 a.m. and 2:00 a.m. the bus arrived on prison grounds.

The large grass lawns of the prison were beautiful. It was still dark, but being much closer, the prison was a lot easier to see. Twenty-four hours earlier McVeigh was able to look up at the moon for the first time in a number of years. This occurred when he was being transported. Sometimes the moon can look more beautiful than normal. Now twenty-four hours later, this was one of those occasions. During this dark morning wait my thoughts were constantly on McVeigh. What was he doing? What is he thinking? Is he really as prepared for death as he seems? Is he scared? Is he despondent? Is he sorry?

How difficult it must be to prepare yourself to see the moon one last time!

On the prison grounds, hay bales had been placed in a circle. The area was made up of a small crowd of people who were also allowed on prison grounds in protest of the execution. A young girl walked around with a Bible in her hand. After sitting on the hay for a short time, I decided to take a quick nap. A couple hundred feet away was a tent. The grass under the tent didn't have dew on it. Finding a large Amnesty International banner, Bill and I spread it out and took a nap. We awoke at 5:00 a.m. It was now light. Standing there the prison could clearly be seen in all its strange glory. At 4:12 a.m. a hundred sixty-eight minutes of silence had started. Waking to the daylight, the prison and the circle of silent witnesses provided a mixture of emotions and senses. Strongest was the thought a man was within an hour of being strapped onto a gurney to await execution. The proximity to the event made the reality and sadness of the lives ruined by this tragedy, including McVeigh's, loom large in my mind.

In the time leading up to the execution, many observations were to be had. There were some protestors who simply thought the federal government executing anyone was unconstitutional. One person thought the whole thing a conspiracy. "Remember WACO" he said.

Beginning at 5:00 a.m., I looked at my watch often. At 6:00 a.m. it was time to strap McVeigh to the gurney. He would lie there for one hour. I looked toward the prison. Between 6:00 and 7:00 a.m. the number of press in the area greatly increased. More people were standing out on Route 63 and traffic increased to a steady pace. As 7:00 a.m. approached, I found myself near the circle of silent witnesses looking in the direction of the death chamber. The 168 minutes of silence came to an end. The people stood and their focus shifted to McVeigh. A minister gave an amazing prayer that captured perfectly how the anti-death proponents felt. Listening in silence, I stood facing the prison and the execution building. The silence of the small crowd was as loud as anything I have ever heard. The morning dew still lingered on the beautiful field of grass as very early morning disappeared into a more reasonable time. The protestors' solemn vigil turned more into sadness as the hopelessness of their cause met reality. An American flag blew strongly in the wind just near the execution chamber; its beauty blowing in strong contrast to the sad story coming to an end. For twenty minutes I stood in silence, facing the prison, listening to the prayers on my right and to my back. The circle of demonstrators started to quietly sing "We Shall Overcome." The silence in the prison yard was still deafening. While I stood in the green grass of the prison field, it was reported in the media that McVeigh came into the view of the witnesses in the execution chamber. Lying on the gurney with a neatly folded sheet pulled up to his chest and a white tee shirt, McVeigh looked at the few witnesses he requested and trusted. Next he looked at the 10 media witnesses one by one, nodding as he made eye contact. He then tried to see the victim witnesses behind the one way glass. He couldn't make eye contact with these witnesses after squinting to see. McVeigh then rested his head on the gurney, looking straight into the ceiling camera sending his picture back to witnesses in Oklahoma City. He made no final word and just stared at the camera. His eyes moved side to side. According to the witness Russ Huppke of the Associated Press, "his chest moved up and down his lips twice puffed out air, as he was fighting to maintain consciousness." At 7:10 a.m. the first drug was administered. Huppke reported, "McVeigh's eyes remained open, but they began to glass over, started to roll up slightly. His pale skin started to turn slightly yellow, almost jaundiced." At 7:11 a.m.

the second drug was administered. Two minutes later the third. Over the next minute, Huppke says, "McVeigh's lips turn the slightest shade of blue. He was still." His eyes remained open. He was dead within four minutes of the first drug. [1]

Outside, after 15 minutes, the silence was broken only by a low flying helicopter entering the prison airspace and flying toward the facility. Word spread through the crowd almost instantly.

Contrary to the rest of the small crowd I felt justice had been done. However, it was a somber occasion. Nothing felt good about it. I thought hard about the justice aspect of it. A man had just been killed. As a longtime, but passive, supporter of the death penalty, good people deeply affected by the morning's event surrounded me. I couldn't help but think about how such a seemingly nice, normal guy could turn so evil. I had no real symphony for Timothy McVeigh on this morning in Terre Haute, but felt no joy in his execution either. I just wanted to go home and hug my kids.

On the bus back to Fairbanks Park I talked to a priest from Michigan who was sitting in front of me. He was against the death penalty. I told him about observing good people on both sides of the issue and he agreed but called the proponents misguided. McVeigh had been dead for half an hour. I asked him where Timothy McVeigh was right now. He said he doesn't know for sure, but thinks he is in heaven. God is forgiving, he added.

Now eleven years later, I am struck even more by these words. In 2011, I lost my first born son, Andrew who was killed in a freak accident while away at college. He embodied goodness. Timothy McVeigh forgiven in Heaven with my son!! It can't be, can it? I go on because of the belief Andrew is in heaven and we will see each other again. I was raised to believe in Hell, but as an adult question its existence. Forgiveness and repentance is a key part of my faith, but I wish there was a Hell for people like Timothy McVeigh. I just don't know if it really exists as a place. The McVeigh execution story is about forgiveness, revenge, justice, and faith. I prefer a Heaven where Andrew is with his Grandfathers, one he never knew. It is all hard for me to justify.

Forgiveness is hard. Revenge is easy. Justice is a necessary part of law. Faith is glorious. According to Edmund Burke, "justice is itself the great standing policy of civil society; and any eminent departure from it, under any circumstances, lies under the suspension of no policy at all." [2] However, Emerson says, one man's justice is another man's injustice." [3] This was evident this sad and confusing day in Terre Haute. With all that said, I don't forgive McVeigh's brand of hate but have no thoughts of revenge either. Was justice done? I guess so. I can only assume McVeigh didn't repent or ask for forgiveness. His soul must be somewhere besides Heaven? If there are no consequences to how you live your life on Earth, what's the point?

Heaven must be a glorious place. It is a place of angels, perhaps as Kris Kristofferson says, "a hall of angels." [4] The thought this evil man could be in heaven is disturbing. I refuse to believe it. The thing most central to my faith makes me question it the most.

1. Russ Huppke, Associated Press, June 12, 2001
2. Reflections on the Revolutions in France, 1790; the Works of the Right Honorable Edmund Burke (1899)
3. Circles, Ralph Waldo Emerson, 1841
4. Hall Of Angels, Jody Richardson Publishing

CHAPTER THREE

DOOLITTLE RAIDERS 57TH REUNION

One thing that doesn't apply to America is to say we have no heroes. As the German poet Bertolt Brecht says "unhappy the land that is in need of heroes."[1] In my mind there are no greater heroes than the Doolittle Raiders. You may ask, "Who are the Doolittle Raiders?" Let me summarize their story and, in particular, the story of Jacob DeShazer.

In 1941, President Roosevelt, following the Japanese attack on Pearl Harbor, demanded the United States bomb the country of Japan as soon as possible. Roosevelt felt it was important for public morale to bomb Japan. This would be no easy task. To lead and plan the attack, he selected the great Jimmy Doolittle. In his autobiography, Doolittle said:

"The Japanese people had been told they were invincible---an attack on the Japanese homeland would cause confusion in the minds of the Japanese people and sow doubt about the reliability of their leaders. There was a second, and equally important psychological reason for the attack---Americans badly needed a morale boost."[2]

Jimmy Doolittle was an American hero, serving in both World Wars. During his long Air Force career he received the Medal of Honor, the Distinguished Service Medal, the Silver Star, and the Distinguished Flying Cross. He served from 1917 through 1959. Doolittle died at the age of 96 in 1993.

On April 18, 1942, just four months after Pearl Harbor, sixteen medium bombers, Mitchell B-25s to be exact, took off from the USS Hornet. They were about 600 miles from Japan and did not have enough fuel to return. Their goal was to bomb Japan and then reach the safe parts of China not controlled by the Japanese. All 16 planes bombed their targets and all except one had to crash land or bail out of the planes. In most cases they had no idea when they were jumping out of their plane whether they were over water or land. Eighty men took part in the raid, five men in each of 16 planes. Of the 80 men, 67 escaped capture and were not killed. All of the Raiders volunteered for this mission. They left with little chance of safe return. The weather was bad and they didn't have enough fuel to return. It was dark and a six hour trip to Japan and their chance of capture was excellent. If not for a tail wind, none would have made it to the safe parts of China after bombing Japan.

Beginning a couple years after the raid, the Doolittle Raiders started an annual reunion that continues to this day. I have attended three of the reunions and my first was the 57th. The highlight of each reunion is where they toast their fellow Raiders who have passed away during the last year. Eighty special engraved silver goblets are used for this toast. "The goblets of those who have died are inverted. So that each crewmember can be recognized, whether dead or alive, their names are engraved on the goblets twice. Right side up and upside down. When only two Raiders remain alive, they will drink a final toast from a vintage 1896 bottle of Hennessy cognac which has accompanied the goblets to each raider Reunion since 1960. The vintage was chosen because it was the year of Jimmy Doolittle's birth."[3]

I left for the 57th Annual Reunion of the Doolittle Raiders on Saturday, April 17, 1999, around 9:00 a.m. My wife and I dropped the kids off at their grandparents' house where they were going to spend the evening. Arriving at the United States Air Force Museum in Dayton, Ohio, we immediately proceeded to the gift shop to obtain items for autographs. The items purchased were two commemorative reunion stamped envelopes dated April 18, 1999, a print of a B-25 Mitchell in flight, three postcards of a B-25, and a large photograph taken the evening before of all the reunion attendees.

We then went to the autograph line, arriving around 12:15 p.m. The autograph session was scheduled to begin at 1:00 p.m. and the line was very slow moving. However, once we made our way to the autograph tables, it was very enjoyable and fast. The Doolittle Raiders were sitting at tables in a U shape in Kettering Hall. There were twenty-one Raiders attending this reunion. A total of twenty-seven were still living. As of the publication of this book there are five. A lady behind us in line was a volunteer at the Museum. We discussed many things including the

Presidential Plane Collection of the Museum, her career at the
Wright Patterson Air Force Base where she worked for years, the
mural in Kettering Hall of the Wright Brothers Kitty Hawk
Flight, and how she once saw Jimmy Doolittle at the Air Force
Base. The first person in line was David Jones, the pilot on Crew
Number 5. He was trying to hurry the line up because it was
moving so very slow. Ann and I met Travis Hoover, the pilot of
Crew Number 2 that took off right after Doolittle. He offered a
handshake. With him was the widow of Ted Lawson (Ellen),
pilot of Crew number 7, who wrote the book *Thirty Seconds Over
Tokyo*. I obtained her autograph although most people didn't ask
her. We were told she was now dating Travis Hoover. Ann was
getting the print autographed and I was working on the photo and
a commemorative envelope. Jacob DeShazer was another Raider
that stood out because he told Ann he signed the print where he
sat for the long flight to Japan. He was the Bombardier on Crew
number 16. Of all the Raiders DeShazer stands out as the one
with the most memories for me. The reasons will be evident
later. David Thatcher was the flight engineer/gunner for Crew
Number 7. He asked where we were from and discussed being in
Lexington for a previous reunion. I said something about there
being a lot of horses there and he said yes and "some still race." I
mentioned to him I was going to Keeneland the following Friday.
Next to Thatcher was James Doolittle III and the lady behind us
asked him if he was related and he said Doolittle was his Father.
The lady said he was bigger than his father. He responded he has
more hair than his father but wasn't as smart. Howard Sesser,
fight engineer, Crew Number 15, said he was from Louisiana,
and that sometimes the reunions are too far for him to travel. I
generally asked each Raider where they were from in order to
strike up a conversation and had some level of a conversation
with each Raider. There were nineteen of the twenty-one Raiders
attending the reunion that participated in the autograph session.
Later that night I went to the Doolittle Reunion Annual Dinner
back at the museum.

The dinner was preceded by a cocktail hour from 6-7:00 p.m. in
Kettering Hall. I spent most of the cocktail hour talking with a
man from West Virginia and his wife. He worked in Disaster and

Emergency Services for the state. The dinner was going to be held in the modern flight hanger of the museum. I found a table up front to the right of the stage and it was marked for the Reverend Jacob DeShazer. I could not have made a better choice and it was also right in front of the Raider Goblets. As mentioned, goblets have been a Raider tradition. I sat at the table with a couple from West Virginia, a retired history professor from Jackson, Mississippi and his wife. He came because he always wanted to meet a Doolittle Raider.

Each of the raiders were introduced, one by one, and entered from the back of the room. They were escorted to their seats by a military escort. It was a tremendous honor to sit at the same table as DeShazer and his wife. During the national anthem, sung by the audience, I thought how amazing these true heroes were. Jake DeShazer was the bombardier for Crew Number 16 and the pilot was William G. Farrow. After the raid, their plane went the deepest into Chinese Territory, and "by the worst luck imaginable, they jumped out of their plane when the fuel was gone and landed in the great bend of the Yangtze River that the Japanese were holding." The entire crew was captured. Farrow and Flight Engineer/Gunner Harold A Spatz were executed. DeShazer and two other crew members spent the entire war in a Japanese POW camp. During his captivity he was sent to Tokyo and spent 40 months as a POW. Thirty-four of those months were in solitary confinement. Treated horribly, he was sentenced to life in prison. He was rescued at wars end. As a result of his captivity, DeShazer had a religious experience, and became a devout Christian. After the war, he went back to Japan and did missionary work for thirty years. In fact, one of the individuals he converted to Christianity was the man who led the raid on Pearl Harbor. Said well in his Wikipedia entry, "DeShazer, the Doolittle Raider who bombed Nagoya, met Captain Mitsuo Fuchida, who led the attack on Pearl Harbor, becoming close friends. Fuchida became a Christian in 1950 after reading a tract written about DeShazer titled, I Was a Prisoner of Japan, and spent the rest of his life as a missionary in Asia and the United States. On occasion, DeShazer and Fuchida preached together as Christian missionaries in Japan. In 1959,

DeShazer moved to Nagoya to establish a Christian church in the city he had bombed" [4]

All the Doolittle raiders volunteered without knowing what their mission was going to be. According to the history books, they had no idea their mission was to bomb Japan until they were out to sea and on the way. I asked DeShazer if they ever figured out what their mission was before being told. He said "No, they fooled us." They first sent us to Charleston, South Carolina and "We thought we were going to Germany." However, he said, our orders sent us to San Francisco. On the way out we flew very low. When seeking volunteers, according to DeShazer, military officers came into a room and said they needed volunteers and some of you "will get killed." He was the fourth one asked. Everyone in front of him said yes and he couldn't be the first to say no, because he didn't want to "be seen as a coward." The novelist Brian Moore said "The world's made up of individuals who don't want to be heroes." This so applied to the Doolittle Raiders. [5]

DeShazer passed away on March 15, 2008. He lived in Oregon and drove all the way to this reunion because he wanted to go to Arkansas. His wife said this may be their last reunion. Later he sent me a copy of his book on his experiences.

Meeting so many of the Doolittle Raiders is one of the great experiences of my life and in particular Jake DeShazer. DeShazer is a hero of mine because his inspirational story is one of bravery, love of country, forgiveness, and faith. I remember a certain sadness when learning of his death. His family of course mourned this great man. However, like all heroes, it is his life that mattered. As General Patton said, "It is foolish and wrong to mourn the men who died. Rather we should thank God that such men lived." [6]

The "Oregon War Veterans Association (OWVA) nominated DeShazer for the Presidential Medal of Freedom and the Congressional Gold Medal noting his extraordinary impact on America as a war hero and for his heroic service to the people of Japan, where he is well known as a hero of peace and reconciliation." OWVA's Executive Director, Greg Warnock also "nominated Rev. DeShazer for the Congressional Gold Medal. In the official nomination letters Warnock wrote, "At this time in our history, we feel it is ideal to honor a man who was a genuine war hero, [but] who after his sacrificial service put on gloves of peace, and touched the entire world with grace and humility." [7]

A warrior, called to action, he put on the "gloves of peace" after doing his duty. He really was a great man, as were so many of that generation.

1.   *The Life of Galileo (1939 Translated Howard Brenton,1980)*
2.   *I Could Never be so Lucky Again, Doolittle and Glines*
3.   *Doolittle Raid, Wikipedia*
4.   *From Bombs to Something More Powerful[dead link].*
      Dealing with the day of Infamy, Cox News, 7 December 2000

      Beyond Pearl Harbor, ChristianHistory.net, 8 August 2008

5.   *Sunday Times April 15, 1990*
6.   *Speech at Copley Plaza Hotel Boston, June 7, 1945*
7.   *Wikipedia, Jake DeShazer Entry.*

CHAPTER FOUR

THE IMPEACHMENT AND TRIAL OF BILL CLINTON

IMPEACHMENT

Let me start by saying I was wrong. On December 19, 1998 the United States House of Representative impeached President William Jefferson Clinton. The buildup to this event had been going on for months. It was in January, 1998, as humorist Dave Berry said, we learned that "Monica Lewinsky worked on the presidential staff." [1] I was caught up in the hoopla and agreed at the time the President should be impeached. He was morally bankrupt but more importantly lied under oath. It was a small lie, but a lie nevertheless. What really pissed me off was the lie to the American people and to his Cabinet. The way he brought his Cabinet out to the White House lawn to back up his lie was reprehensible.

If you assume a hooker would charge $65 for a blow job, and let's say Clinton received six. Who really knows how many but six would be a good month. At $65 each that would be a total of $395 (Based upon prices at the Mustang Ranch outside Reno in the 1980's when the federal government took over ownership. Before you think it, I just asked and didn't touch the merchandise. I just had to visit a government owned brothel. Too good of a story to pass up.) A total of $395 would be a small claims court issue. Of course, Monica Lewinsky was not a hooker and was a young lady taken advantage of and actually sexually harassed when looking at how she was treated professionally after the affair ended. After seven years of throwing everything at this president, Clinton finally gave the Republicans something they could really use. So much so they could even impeach him. Only Andrew Johnson had been impeached before and in that case he was doing the right thing. At least with Clinton he really screwed up and lied under oath. This historic impeachment debate and the trial in the United States Senate could not be passed up.

Twenty-five years earlier the country had been talking
Impeachment and if he hadn't resigned, Richard Nixon would
have become the second president in history to be impeached.
Instead that honor went to Bill Clinton. As a lover of history,
even as a child, I had known about the Impeachment of Andrew
Johnson. The founding fathers had a good idea—a nonpartisan
process for removing the President for "high crimes and
misdemeanors." The House of Representatives would consider
Impeachment and the Senate would then try the President and if
found guilty he would be removed from office. Like Bill
Clinton, Johnson didn't get along with the Republicans in the
House. They didn't trust his authority since he assumed the
Vice-presidency following the assassination of Lincoln. In
particular the "radical Republicans disliked Johnson. He asserted
his power by firing the popular Edwin M. Stanton, Secretary of
War. This really angered Congress. [2] Thus Congress passed the
Tenure in Office Act, prohibiting the President from firing any
official who had been appointed with the consent of the Senate.
Obviously unconstitutional, it meant the President couldn't fire
any member of his Cabinet without first getting the approval of
the Senate. However, the stage was set for Impeachment.
Stanton who got his job back under the law, was fired a second
time. On February 24, 1868, Congress introduced eleven Articles
of Impeachment. Johnson would be on trial in the Senate.

Because of the courage of one Senator, Edmund G. Ross, the last
undecided vote, Johnson was acquitted by one vote. The entire
event was political and based more on a dislike of Johnson than
any specific crime committed. Ross, from Kansas, had voted to
acquit Johnson and as a result, lost his seat two years later.
President John F. Kennedy selected Ross as one of eight
Senators to highlight in his Book "Profiles in Courage," which
discussed acts of courage in the Senate that Kennedy thought
inspiring.

Fast forward to 1998. The Republicans disliked Bill Clinton
politically and personally and did so since the day he took office.
He was investigated more than any President and was largely
untouched. It seemed with Clinton it was much more than

political differences. It seemed like hatred. Much the same way Democrats would feel toward George W. Bush a few years later.

In the midst of that hatred, Bill Clinton gave the Republicans the greatest weapon from which to attack—a new and improved scandal. In Nixon's case, impeachment would have been deserved and in following with the intent of the Constitution. It was not in Johnson's case. Bill Clinton lied under oath, giving the Republicans some point for impeachment.

The worst part of it all to me was that Bill Clinton was so distrustful. He lied to us so often about his adultery. Most of us would lie about adultery. However, he was running for the presidency when he lied during the famous 60 minutes episode. Then came the great "I did not have sex with that woman, Ms. Lewinsky." We all knew he was lying. As Jerry Seinfeld said, "Everyone lies about sex. Without lying there'd be no sex." [3]

The charges against Clinton centered on the Starr Report and most compelling was the perjury charges. However, was it Impeachable?

I first talked about going to Washington in January when Sam Donaldson of ABC News said the President would resign within a week of the scandal breaking. How wrong he was! The Judiciary Committee hearing began in the fall. I had planned to leave for DC on December 17,1998 to attend the first day of the Impeachment hearing of the full House of Representatives. My anticipation built throughout the morning. However, shortly after lunch, rumors started to fly that the United States was going to take military action against Iraq for violating the terms of the cease fire of the Persian Gulf War. Before the day was over, the bombing started and the Impeachment debate was off. My flight reservations were cancelled. However, it was quickly decided the Impeachment hearings would start the next day, Friday December 18, 1998. I remember promising my two sons to take them to the Cincinnati Zoo for the holiday Festival of Lights tradition. Flight reservations were made for 6:25 a.m. the next morning. Perhaps my wife should have impeached me for leaving two days before the entire side of my family would be at our house for a Christmas party. Did I say I love you Ann?

Arriving in Baltimore on schedule, a taxi was taken into Washington. The country was going about its business as if nothing out of the ordinary was taking place. In my mind, the most historic event of my life was about to start. In DC, I immediately went to the office of Congressman Jim Bunning to obtain passes to the hearing and then sprinted to the House Chambers not wanting to waste any precious time. I was as excited as I have been at any historic event. It doesn't get any better than this was my mindset.

I quickly positioned myself in the line just as Indiana Congressman Lee Hamilton passed me. Hamilton served as Congressman from 1965 to 1999 and would serve as vice –chair of the 9/11 Commission a couple years later. Today, he serves on the Homeland Security Advisory Council. It was a cold December day but the weather was the last thing on my mind. History was my blanket. At approximately 9:10 a.m., I walked into the House Gallery. Upon entering, I saw Representative Henry Hyde sitting down after introducing the motion to impeach. I took my seat directly behind the Republican side of the chamber. Hyde, the Congressman from Illinois, served as the Chair of the House Judiciary Committee from 1995 until 2001. His biggest claim to fame was in this role because he became the Republican point person in the impeachment of President Clinton. He died in 2007. As we watched him sit down, according to U.S. House of Representatives records, Hyde had just said, "What we are telling you today are not the ravings of some vast right wing conspiracy, but a reaffirmation of a set of values that are tarnished and dim these days, but it is given to us to restore them so the founding fathers would be proud. It's your country—the President is the flag bearer, out in front of our people. The flag is falling, my friends-I ask you to catch the falling flag as we keep our appointment with history."

The Clerk of the House of Representatives then read the Articles of Impeachment. I literally had a chill run down my body and sat there in awe of the historical event being witnessed. Two charges of perjury, obstruction of justice, and abuse of power! I have been present at many historical events and none have stood out like this one. The Gallery sat in complete silence. The history of the event could be "felt" as the clerk read the Articles of Impeachment. Representative Hyde then spoke and gave an incredible speech. The quote that stood out to me was "My colleagues, we have been sent here to strengthen and defend the rule of law, not to weaken it, not to attenuate it, not to disfigure it. This is not a question of perfection; it is a question of Foundations." Next to speak was Missouri Representative Richard Gephardt who eloquently spoke out against Impeachment. Gephardt, the House Minority leader said his concerns were the Republicans were not allowing a vote on censure. He said, "You get to vote your vote of conscience and I respect that right. All we're asking is that we get to vote our conscience." The only time both sides of the aisle were observed cheering at the same time was when Gephardt made a remark against the politics of smear. I spent two hours in the chamber before being rotated out. It was the most historic time of the day to be in the chamber. Outside it was bitterly cold.

Outside the capital, I visited one of my favorite spots—where John Wilkes Booth stood during Lincoln's second Inauguration just a few weeks before the assassination. Mingling among a handful of protestors on the east side of the stately capitol building was exciting. There were not many people, but all were opposed to Impeachment. It was surprising to me how few people were protesting this historic occasion. Standing there observing, David Maraniss, Clinton's biographer, walked past me. He won a Pulitzer Prize for his coverage of the 1992 Clinton campaign and today continues to work for *The Washington Post*. Talking to him briefly, he was embarrassed when I sought his autograph. As a collector of historic manuscripts, I always try to obtain an autograph. I also talked with West Virginia Representative Bob Wise who was holding a press conference. Like all Representatives, we spoke with Wise and he told me how well he understood the gravity of his vote and the historic significance of the time. He would vote to impeach. Later Wise would serve as the 33rd Governor of West Virginia.

After talking with Congressman Wise, I went back to the House Chamber again. One of the best speeches was from Representative Peter King of New York. Congressman King said

he was against impeachment. A total of five Republicans
eventually voted against. To me, it appeared King showed a lot
of guts to do what he did. The pressure from the Republicans
was tremendous. It was pretty clear Clinton was in trouble in the
House. King did, however, once call the President's conduct
"illegal and irresponsible." Just after his speech, outside the
Capitol, I saw Representative King and told him how much I
admired what he did on the House floor. King was with
Congressman Amo Houghton (R-NY) who also would vote
against impeachment. Was King the Edmund Ross of this
century? King continues to serve his New York District and has
done so since 1993. Today, he is no longer an obscure
Congressman, serving as Chair of the House Committee on
Homeland security.

In this area, where we saw King, was a section of the capitol
lawn set aside for press conferences. A podium was set up and
this is where Congressmen would announce how they planned on
voting. Congressman Frank Riggs (R-CA) held a press
conference announcing his intention to vote for impeachment.
Riggs said," A majority of Americans now believe that President
Clinton lied to us and damaged the basic trust between the
American people and their President. Just as seriously, if the
American people do not believe that President, why should our
allies or our enemies. I believe the President can no longer
effectively perform the duties and responsibilities for which he
was elected. For the good of the country, he should resign, as I
have said for months." In closing his remarks, Riggs said "I will
vote to impeach William Jefferson Clinton." [3] Standing right
next to me was a man who, when Riggs announced his intentions,
yelled "Shame, shame on you." As he was hauled away by the
police, he yelled "I thought this was a free country." This was a
great moment. Each of these Congressmen would be voting in an
attempt to impeach the President of the United States. Inside the
House Chamber, all the events were recorded; preserved for
history. Outside, people like me were roaming around. Second
to being in the House, this was my favorite spot to be. I love the
nuances of history; the small events witnessed by people that

otherwise would be lost to history. I was the equivalent of a patron in Ford's Theater on April 14, 1865.

Being hungry, I ate in the House of Representatives Office Building Cafeteria. However, why not incorporate a little history in the walk to the cafeteria. On the way back from eating, a stop by Room 2141 of the Rayburn Office Building was in order. This is not only the room of the Judiciary Committee where impeachment hearings were recently held, but the site of the Watergate Hearings. The doors were locked. The next stop before going back to the House Chambers was the office of Henry Hyde which is near Room 2141. The receptionist was away from her desk, but there was a secret service agent posted at the office. He asked if we "were from Illinois". I said "no," but we just wanted to stop by Congressman Hyde's office on this historic day. Should have said "yes"! He didn't see things the same way I did. I left on his instruction.

Back to the House Chamber for round three. This was the longest time to stand in line all day, about 45 minutes. In line was a military officer in charge of nationwide advertising for the National Guard and a teacher from Louisiana. Like me they couldn't pass up this historic opportunity. This time my visit in the Gallery lasted one hour and it was dominated by more speeches for and against impeachment. Upon leaving, I decided to go back one more time and was in almost immediately. Part of the reason to go back was Congressman Jim Bunning, my representative, was getting close to his speech but I had to leave the gallery by 7:15 p.m. to get back to Baltimore. Congressman Bunning was called around 7:00 p.m. To my disappointment he did not speak, but simply handed his remarks to the clerk. Bunning wound up in a unique place in history. He voted to impeach Clinton in the House of Representatives. However, he had also just been elected to the United States Senate in November and was now just finishing out his House term. When he took over as Senator in January he voted to convict Clinton during the Senate trial. Two votes, one to impeach and one to convict.

During the day many speeches with some intense debate were heard. Representative Joe Kennedy, the son of Robert Kennedy, gave one of the day's best with passionate remarks. He was one of the few to not use any notes and it was later called in *The Boston Herald* as "an impassioned plea for unity and forgiveness." This was his last ever speech as a Congressman. Luis Stokes, (D-OH), while not a great speech, also gave his last remarks as a Congressman. He was retiring after thirty years in the House. Many Congressmen made their last appearance on the House floor this day. Representative Pat Kennedy made one of the worst presentations. He came across as really immature because he was running through the aisle and seemed to be acting like a child instead of a Congressman. Representative Sam Johnson (R-TX) provided an historic moment. His speech was not great, but during it Henry Hyde came up to the microphone and interrupted to interject that Johnson was a former pilot who was a POW in Vietnam for seven years. Hyde seemed to do this because one of the major themes of the Democrats was the Impeachment Debate should not be going on while our "young men and women" are engaged in a conflict overseas. The Democrats were clearly trying to use the Armed Services for short-term political gain. Sam Johnson, in his remarks said, "Our military fighting men want the Congress to carry on our responsibilities every day." Charles Rangel (D-NY) said the President must be supported during military actions. He said, "You can't salute him in the morning and impeach him in the afternoon." While there is truth to the statement, the Impeachment hearings had begun. When speaker after speaker referenced the "young men and women" of the military as reason to not proceed with impeachment it came across as a new and convenient tool to oppose impeachment. The pettiest moment came when James Sensenbrenner (R-WI) questioned the speaker, Ray LaHood (R-IL), about the amount of time Gephardt had used in his opening remarks.

During the day, a total of five hours was spent in the House Gallery.

At one point in the day, I was interviewed by the *Baltimore Sun* and upon exiting the House Chamber, came across Representative Dick Gephardt at the bottom of the Gallery steps. I remarked about standing near a man who very well could be

President of the United States someday. Gephardt had run in 1988 and would do so again in 2004. He never came close to winning the Presidency.

Catching a 9:30 p.m. flight from Baltimore to Louisville, arriving at 11:10 p.m., I was so thirsty the stewardess brought me seven glasses of water before the flight ever took off. Seeing history can make you thirsty. Following the flight, I drove home and was in bed around 1:30 a.m., an hour and forty minutes short of a twenty-four hour day.

The next day about 21 people on my side of the family came over to celebrate Christmas. Earlier in the day, I watched the President of the United States impeached on television. My wife still loved me and America went on. I can't remember one Christmas gift that year, but can vividly remember my time in DC during the Impeachment Hearings. What seemed like a fair decision now seems like a low point in partisan politics. The nation now had to endure worse----a trial.

CLINTON ON TRIAL

Excited, who would have ever thought I would get to see an Impeachment Trial in my lifetime? I felt like Forrest Gump. As a lover of presidential history, this was the best it could get. If I was to pick an historic event to attend this would be it----except for a tryst between JFK and Marilyn Monroe. Going back in time I, perhaps, would pick the time of Johnson's trial to visit. Today, however, like the Johnson trial, it would show the best and worst of American politics.

I left for the Trial on January 21, 1999 with a friend, Bill Scheyer, and my sister, Janet. For Friday, we had public passes which meant waiting in line For Saturday, we secured one family pass from a connection of Janet's husband at the Republican National Committee. We pulled into DC around three in the afternoon and parked at the Pentagon and took the subway to Capitol Hill. The Capitol City seemed perfectly normal and oblivious to the storm taking place. The RNC referred me to Senator James Jeffords who gave us one family pass for the next day. Washington was crowded because of a massive pro-life rally. It was the anniversary of the Roe v. Wade Supreme Court decision. The crowd was perhaps 100,000. Senator McConnell's office provided passes for Friday and two staff passes for Saturday. We were all set and my excitement was strong. I kept putting this in context of history and the Johnson trial. Upon entering the Senate Chamber, Supreme Court Chief Justice William Rehnquist was sitting in his chair. Our seats were behind the Chief Justice and to his right and in the last row. These were not great seats but I was in the Chamber so it didn't matter. Chief Justice Rehnquist presiding over an Impeachment Trial was almost too much to behold. It was such an exciting historical moment. During the Johnson Trial, Salmon P. Chase presided. He is one of my favorite historical figures, although I don't always agree with him. Chase was born in 1808 and served as a U.S. Senator from Ohio, the 23rd Governor of Ohio, as U.S. Secretary of Treasury under Lincoln, and the sixth Chief Justice of the United States. He was strongly opposed to slavery and is credited with the phrase " free soil, free labor, free men." [4] He was an ardent free soiler. Chase is buried in Spring Grove Cemetery in Cincinnati. Each year around the end of December, Bill Scheyer and I visit the grave of Chase. We have a bottle of wine, a sandwich, leave a rose, and talk over our past year and thoughts for the upcoming year. It is a time of reflection, planning, and rejuvenation. The grave sits on a hill overlooking the beautiful Spring Grove Lake. Usually covered with ice during the cold winter months, the lake is still home to beautiful geese. Each year the scene is the same proving an inspiration to my historic endeavors. It never changes as I age. The annual Chase visit happened just a couple weeks before this current trip to our nation's capital.

William Rehnquist would only live another six years following the Impeachment Trial. He was a strong supporter of the Tenth Amendment concept of federalism and the powers of the states. He and Chase are the only two Supreme Court Chief Justices to preside over a presidential impeachment trial.

We were out of the gallery as the Senate adjourned by 6:05 p.m. When the Senate adjourned we ran into comedian Al Franken who would become a Senator himself in a few years. Ironically, as my friend Kevin Kelly says, "he is funnier as a Senator than he ever was as a comedian." Franken talked with us briefly. The one thing I dislike is those individuals who are not civil and hate people if they disagree with them politically. Al Franken reminds me of such a person. Maybe he has governed better but before becoming a Senator he seemed like a person that hated those who disagreed with him: a Michael Moore type.

After leaving the Capitol, I noticed something going on in front of the Supreme Court and we headed over. Janet, an ardent pro-life person picked up two anti-abortion signs that were on the ground. At the Court, there were about 50 protestors from the National Organization of Women (NOW). They were holding a counter protest to the large pro-life rally earlier in the day. I talked with NOW President Patricia Ireland who spoke to me of "peace and equality." Upon leaving I was confused about what this meant. Her statement was about their pro-choice stance but I never made the connection between "peace, equality, and pro-choice. She served as President of NOW until 2001. Born in 1945, Ireland is one of America's premier feminists.

Walking down the street to a restaurant recommend by a DC police officer, there was a light on in a congressional office. Looking closer I saw a Cincinnati poster on the wall. It was the office of Congressman Steve Chabot, a floor manager for the Impeachment Trial. He had just left the Senate floor. There were 13 floor managers who served as the prosecutors for the trial. Chabot served as a key player in the trial. Never to pass up an opportunity, we quickly made it through the door and into the Cannon Office Building. We went to Chabot's office. The door at 129 Cannon was locked. However, as Bill turned the knob on the door, someone on the other end opened it and it was Congressman Chabot. We talked about the trial with Chabot for about five minutes. He was very proud of his involvement particularly serving as a Floor Manager. It was a great honor. He recognized the tremendous history of the event and felt it was a sad time for the country. We also talked about University of Cincinnati basketball. It was his birthday and he was off to celebrate it over dinner. We had just had a great conversation with a floor manager. We were so excited we floated on air to our restaurant down the street. The night was cold this historic evening and DC was preparing for dinner and the conclusion of another day in the trial of President Clinton. I was so high and seeing history is my drug. Day one couldn't have gone better.

The best place to eat breakfast in Washington is Bob and Edith's Diner in Arlington. It first opened in 1969 and serves the best breakfast, lunch, and dinner. I hate to call it a dive, but I will in the most complimentary way possible. Its uniqueness is what makes it great. This is how day two started out: sausage and eggs at Bob and Edith's. It doesn't get any better.

We arrived at Senator McConnell's office before it opened but staff member Robert Stewart let us in early. He gave us the passes and we asked about the office. We knew it was Richard Nixon's old office which is now full of cubicles. Nixon's fireplace was behind one of the cubicles. We also knew Arizona Senator Barry Goldwater, and former presidential candidate, had his office somewhere in McConnell's suite. It just happened that Goldwater used the same office as McConnell. We went in after Stewart made sure the Senator was not in there. We found our goal—to see the marks on the large wooden front door. Goldwater used to sit at his desk and shoot a bee bee gun at the door. The marks are still there.

We took the congressional subway from Russell Office Building to the Capitol. Janet sat in the family section of the gallery and Bill and I in the staff. The session started around 10:10 a.m. and we were in our seats maybe ten minutes earlier. Again, it was inspiring to watch Chief Justice Rehnquist oversee the trial. He was very patient in allowing people to talk. We sat behind the Democratic section facing front and saw a lot of great testimony. During the Friday session and today's, Senators asked questions in written form through the Chief Justice. The trial adjourned for lunch around12:40 p.m. and we ate in a small cafeteria in the Hart Office Building. On our way back to the gallery, Indiana Senator Richard Lugar bumped into me literally, shoulder to shoulder. Recently, he lost his Senate seat that he held since 1977. Riding the Senate subway, and sitting next to us on our way to lunch, was Senator John Kerry. The Senator was being interviewed and was discussing the morning session. After leaving the subway, we wound up in the elevator with the future Democratic Presidential candidate and current Secretary of State. I tried to speak with him briefly but all he said in a raised voice was "WHAT?" His grand personality shining through!

We made our way into the gallery.

This session lasted until around 3:40 p.m. During it, Rehnquist reversed an earlier ruling he had made because in the Andrew Johnson Impeachment trial he now believed Chase had erred in a statement. Representative Hyde, like in the impeachment hearings, provided some historic moments. He is a great orator and gave one speech that was amazing. The adjournment vote was controversial. There was an objection to adjournment by a Democratic Senator and thus a vote was taken. The majority of Senators, both Democrats and Republicans, voted to adjourn. One of the great things about the trial was observing the Senators. Simply watching their mannerisms, maneuvers, discussions provided such a great feel for the event. As an example, Senator Strom Thurmond walking around was truly historic. This was a man who ran for President in the 50's. Senator Byrd was good to watch and he would vote to acquit the President. However, he seemed to be the only Democrat to keep an open mind during the trial. Of course most Republicans had prejudged the case also. One of the worst moments seemed to come from Thurmond and Jim Bunning when they asked if settling the Paula Jones lawsuit didn't mean the President admits his guilt in that case. I guess they didn't understand the law or how cases are often settled without guilt being admitted.

Before heading out of town, we needed to return the staff's pass to Jeffords' office. Jeffords eventually was one of only five Republicans to vote to acquit the President. I like independent thinkers like Jeffords who is not as partisan. He was forced out of the Republican Party in 2001 and retired from the Senate in 2006. On the way over to his office, I talked with Democratic Senator John Breaux from Louisiana who voted to acquit the President and served in the Senate until 2005. Like most Senators we talked to, Breaux was caught up in the history of the event, but equally aware of the politics of the situation and he was unhappy that the country has found itself in this situation.

On February 12, 1999, the full Senate voted to acquit President Clinton of all charges. Two thirds of the senators, or 67 members, were needed for conviction. Fifty Senators voted to convict on the obstruction charge and 45 on the perjury. They were 17 votes short on the obstruction charge. Not one Democratic Senator voted for guilty. [5]

Of course, all of the impeachment hearings and trial was partisan. The Democrats would in a couple years stonewall everything George W. Bush would do and at every turn scream for bipartisanship. The Republicans did the same thing when Clinton was in office. Both parties are hypocrites. As we know Clinton lied—blatantly to the American people and it was inexcusable. It is a joke anytime I hear of any type of sex scandal against anyone on Capitol Hill. Who gives a crap! The American people decided during the Clinton Presidency that character absolutely doesn't matter when it comes to politics. Clinton set a horrible precedent for the measure of anyone with their eye on the Presidency.

Two months following the trial, Clinton was cited by a federal judge for civil contempt for his "willful failure" to obey her repeated orders to testify truthfully in the Paula Jones case. He was fined $90,000 and the case referred to the Arkansas Supreme Court for disciplinary action. The judge said, "simply put, the President's disposition regarding whether he had ever been alone with Ms. Lewinsky was intentionally false, and his statements regarding whether he ever engaged in sexual relations with Ms. Lewinski likewise were intentionally false." [6]

We knew this all along. However, I am now glad we found him innocent. Let me ask: Would the Democrats and Republicans have had the exact opposite opinions if the fortunes had been reversed? If so, that makes the whole impeachment trial a partisan affair. Henry Hyde would have opposed the impeachment of a Republican President in the same set of circumstances. House Democrats would have impeached a Republican had they been in power and the same thing happened. No doubt!! This tells us all we need to know. Yes, Clinton gave them cause but I can't help believe we can do better as a nation in terms of getting along. Both parties refuse to work together and it seems like the modern bickering between the two parties started by the Republicans during the Clinton Administration. Of course, the Democrats continued it with their treatment of Bush. At least in Johnson's Impeachment Trial, there were Statesmen, such as Ross. In Clinton's there was no such thing.

1. *Dave Berry, 1999*
2. *Steven Barr, Washington Post, November 30, 1998*
3. *Press release, Congressman Frank Riggs, December 18, 1998*
4. *Wikipedia Salmon P. Chase.*
5. *Wikipedia, Impeachment of Bill Clinton*
6. *Wikipedia, Impeachment of Bill Clinton*

CHAPTER FIVE
IOWA CAUCUS

I have attended two Iowa Caucuses and in each case spent the
week before following campaigns around the state. In both
instances, I went to a caucus on election night. Visiting the
caucuses is an experience every political scientist or historian
should do. How important are the caucuses really? Well, it
depends. It certainly can spring board a candidate to the
nomination or more than likely end a campaign before it barely
gets started. Let me relate one story from 2000 that helps show
the beauty of this unique type of election.

In 2000, the caucus I attended was at Valley High School in West
Des Moines. The registered voters of each precinct go to one
location for a caucus and each party has their own. I attended a
Democratic caucus because in 2000 the Republicans were using
secret ballots and it wasn't as exciting. The Democratic caucus
would have supporters for the various candidates break in to
groups. The caucus I attended had 48 people attend. They
counted the attendees and I was announced as an observer. After
the count and some small business, the attendees broke into three
sections as follows: Bill Bradley - 30 people, Al Gore - 17
people, and undecided - 1 person. I was standing in the front of
the room with the leader of the caucus. Now keep in mind,
ultimately, the purpose of the caucus is to assign candidate
delegates to the county conventions and then eventually the state
convention. Based upon the numbers supporting each candidate,
they assigned the precincts five delegates. Three went to Bradley
and two to Gore. These again were delegates to the county
convention. The reason Gore received a second delegate was
because of rounding—his rounding being closer to .5. A
Bradley supporter requested permission to talk with the one
undecided person in order to convince her to come to their side.
A Gore supporter did the same. They all huddled in a corner of
the room. The group included the voter, the Gore supporter, the
Bradley supporter, and as observers me and my friend, Bill. It
was very interesting to watch this process close up and the
undecided person was a young girl of seventeen. A person had to

be eighteen by the date of the general election to participate in the caucus. After five minutes of both sides trying to sell her on their candidate, she decided to go with Bradley. This changed the delegate count from 3-2 to 4-1 Bradley. This seventeen year old girl, individually, cost Gore a delegate.

Once the voting was concluded, the caucus considered resolutions sent down from the Democratic Party. However, the group had some resolutions of their own to consider. Different citizens introduced and the group discussed and adopted resolutions against school vouchers, three pro positions on gay rights, and one on green space preservation.

The entire process was very interesting; especially, to watch one seventeen year old girl swing an entire delegate.

In 2012 my son, Ethan, and I attended a Republican caucus at an elementary school in West Des Moines. Upon arrival, we explained about wanting to observe and they were very cordial. We helped set up chairs and we sat at a table and talked to the people about the caucus. One young lady at our table was caucusing for the first time and like so many Iowans was glad the caucus had finally arrived. By the time it does, Iowans are ready for the caucuses to be over, having endured presidential candidates for two years. Ron Paul supporters arrived early and were organized and they put a flyer out at each table and had signs. At our caucus, only three people spoke: for Paul, Rick Santorum, and Mitt Romney. They all did well. The caucus included the pledge of allegiance, election of caucus chair and secretary, passing out an envelope to collect money to help pay for party expenses in holding the caucus, speeches, and then the vote. Small paper ballots were distributed to people when they arrived and showed proof of residency. One person for each candidate had five minutes to talk. There were two for Paul and they had to agree who would talk. The one who didn't later tried to talk and was not allowed. Finally, votes were made and turned in and Paul won this caucus. Ethan was quite impressed with the caucus and said all elections should be like this. I don't know about that, but it is easy to get caught up in the uniqueness of a caucus.

Visiting the Iowa caucuses provides a tremendous perspective on
this unique event. It is difficult to really understand just how a
caucus works without attending one. I have been very impressed
both times sitting through a caucus in Iowa. In Kentucky, all we
have to do is quickly vote. At a caucus, the participant gives up a
night away from home. The voters are more engaged. Most
Americans would never give up the time it takes to caucus. Iowa
should be very proud of its role in the presidential election and
that it takes this role so seriously. Many a candidate has had their
dreams dashed in the cornfields of Iowa. Many more obscure
politicians have been launched to the presidency or to serious
contender status overnight. Overnight, of course, is a completely
false statement. I have learned Iowa is a grassroots state.
Candidates do not win Iowa without spending a year there. They
have to meet each voter three or more times. Each voter will
meet every candidate in person. The candidates have to appear at
endless diners, pizza parlors, and other places the voters go.
Spend a year in Iowa, make 400 campaign appearances, and they
might - just might - win the caucus and go on to New Hampshire.

CHAPTER SIX

AL GORE DIDN T EAT THE MACCARONI

It was bitterly cold as Bill Scheyer and I pulled into the Town
Square of Newton, Iowa. At the time. Newton was home to
Maytag prior to being bought by Whirlpool and relocated. It was
a couple days before the 2000 Iowa Caucuses and Al Gore would
be doing a rally at a union hall in Newton. Following a brief
security check, we were in the hall. The room was set up with
tables across the room going all the way to the back. The press
was located in the back of the room. We didn't realize it, but it
was a pot luck event. People were bringing good old home
cooking dishes into the event. We were in the middle of America
and it felt great. We sat across from four very nice ladies and one
elderly man. We had a great conversation about both Iowa and
Kentucky and connected as individuals from two predominately
rural states.

Al Gore speaks at Union Hall in Newton, IA in 2000

Al Gore entered the room with a pie he took to the food table. He
then immediately came to us and shook our hands. We
welcomed him and the Vice President then worked the rest of the
room. He came back to our area and we shook hands a second
time and had our pictures taken. We told him we were from
Kentucky. Gore then went to the food line, picked up his food,

and grabbed a seat a few feet from us. He had a diet coke and chicken. After eating, Gore stood up to speak and acknowledged his friends from Kentucky and that he appreciates all we are doing for him. The Vice President gave a very good stump speech. He spoke fluently, had a good grasp of his materials, and rolled into an increased tone toward a highly charged close. He ended by saying, "I am going to fight for you. Will you fight for me?" Gore signed my commemorative invitation from his first inauguration, and worked his way back to the bus. After the event, I noticed Gore's Diet Coke can still sitting by his plate and thought what a great souvenir. I went to get it and a woman started to take it. "I'll take this", I said. The can is still proudly displayed in my home office.

However, what about the macaroni? During his speech, Gore said how good the food was and he particularly liked the macaroni. I watched him get his food and eat it. He did not have any macaroni!!

Why would he not tell the truth about the macaroni? They say follow the money to find the truth. Were the macaroni lobby a big contributor to the Gore campaign? Was this another Clinton era scandal that the left wing media would let slide? Let's give him the benefit of the doubt. Remember when George H.W. Bush said, "I do not like broccoli," and the political fallout from the broccoli loving public. Gore probably just wanted the macaroni vote even if he had to fudge the truth about it.

CHAPTER SEVEN

*THE WORST THING I SAW DURING THE 2000
PRESIDENTIAL ELECTION*

During the 2000 presidential election, I traveled approximately 15,000 miles following presidential candidates from probably ten different political parties. The worst thing I saw was at the very first event I attended in Iowa at the Caucuses.

On January 22, I attended a Rally at a church in Des Moines called "A Presidential Rally for Family, Faith, and Freedom." This was a rally for socially conservative individuals and candidates on the anniversary of the Roe V. Wade decision legalizing abortion in America. One year earlier I was at the Clinton impeachment trial. This rally allowed me to meet many presidential candidates including Alan Keyes, Steve Forbes, Gary Bauer, and Howard Phillips from the Constitution Party. This was a conservative event where George Bush was described as a "pretender" on the abortion issue. Georgia Congressman Bob Barr spoke as did Phyllis Schlafly, founder of the Eagle Forum, a conservative interest group. Barr, later, was the Libertarian Party nominee for President in 2008. He was a floor manager in the Clinton impeachment hearings and introduced the resolution asking the House Judiciary Committee to investigate the Impeachment of Clinton.

Michael Johnson was gay, HIV positive, born again, and no longer engaged in homosexual behavior. Fine---those are his choices in life. He spoke on his Christian beliefs. For this his mother was proud. Francis Johnson spoke of how proud she was of her son because "he is no longer a practicing homosexual." She stated she could not love her son while he was engaged in homosexual activity and was not there for him when he was a young man. Now she loves him and is proud. I was struck by how sad it is for a mother to have such conditional love for her child. A parent to put such limitations on the love of their child is so sad and pathetic. In fact it is unnatural. As Author Ann Brashares says, "Parents were the only one obligated to love you; from the rest of the world you had to earn it." [1] Is not the love of a mother to a child supposed to be the greatest love of all? It is not by being a parent that you learn unconditional love?

Obviously, parents have different sets of emotions when a child comes out. I wouldn't know from experience. However, your child isn't any different when they come out. In the book, *Always My Child*, Kevin Jennings says "character is not defined by what you are but by who you are: Are you hard working? Do you treat other people respectfully? Do you have integrity? These qualities do not change because your child comes out."[2]

"The greatest gift that you can give to others is the gift of unconditional love and acceptance." [3]

1.   *Amy Brashares, Forever in Blue: The Forth Summer of the Sisterhood.*
2.   *Always my Child, Kevin Jennings, Fireside Press, 2003*
3.   *Brian Tracy, http://www.brainyquote.com*

CHAPTER EIGHT

THE US PACIFIST PARTY

This nation really needs a Third Party. In many ways there is not a real difference between the Republicans and Democrats. The left and the right are a sham of the two-party system. The left-right paradigm seems like an illusion. Republicans and Democrats are two sides of the same coin. Even if there are policy differences, they do have one thing in common---complete and utter incompetence. Look at what they have done together to this great nation and look how they put party above country. My own United States Senator Mitch McConnell said his number one priority was to make sure Barack Obama is a one-term president. Well he failed at that and he failed the American people. His priority was not the deficit, the constitution, jobs, foreign policy, or protection of liberties. It was the defeat of the president. We, the American people, are all losing because of these parties, one of which I am a member. All they care about is re-election and nothing ever changes because of their desire to stay in power.

Third parties are discriminated against by the mainstream parties. They have different signature requirements to get on state ballots, as well as, many other discriminatory rules. They can't participate in debates because of the rules established by the Republicans and Democrats. For example, unless they are polling a certain percentage of the electorate, they are not allowed in the debates. I am ok with this. However, why can't the Commission on Presidential Debates hold a debate for third party candidates? The reason, the commission is dominated by Republicrats.

During the 2000 presidential election, I followed third party candidates and attended many national events. These parties included the Natural Law Party, the Constitution Party, the Green Party, the Libertarian Party, and the Pacifist Party. All of these are well established political parties except the US Pacifist Party. I found them all interesting, but was also intrigued by a party started, in part, because of a mathematical formula. Let me say before going on, there are many reputable third parties. This one really isn't one but I found it interesting.

I had a conversation with Bradford Lyttle, the Presidential candidate of the United States Pacifist Party. Lyttle was the Presidential candidate for the party in 1984, 1996, 2000, and 2012. Lyttle received degrees from three universities and founded the party in 1983. On the cold fall Chicago day we talked, Lyttle had still gone sailing out on the lake. The Chicago summer was warm but now the fall was cold. His view was the military establishment is contrary to the moral principles of the nine great religions. In 2000, the party web page said "the party is designed to give expression within a democratic, electoral context to the belief that military power profoundly contradicts many religious and philosophic principles and is a practical mistake in our time." It sees "military traditions and institutions as the key obstacle to the solution of major social evils, such as war and the arms race, poverty and political oppression." Lyttle and the party believe the notion that the military system can be made stable is wrong. As any political science student knows, the traditional thinking is that a balance of power can be established between nations militarily. If the nations are similar in strength; war can be averted. Lyttle says, "Large systems cannot be stable forever. No political science is airtight." The party is based upon a scientific foundation. This foundation is important because you can't make a "dent without scientific philosophy" in changing people's beliefs. Thus he created the "Apocalypse Equation (AE)." In essence, the equation is based upon his logic that you can make a reasonable assumption of a nuclear holocaust. If a guy plays Russian roulette every half hour, he always has a five in six chance of surviving. However, at some point he is going to die. How long? We don't know, but it is going to happen. Any other belief is "wishful thinking."

Lyttle says we might consider the chance of the accidental launch of a strategic missile. A form of the AE that lends itself to this simple algebra:

$$AP = 1 - (1 - p(U+S))^n$$

"Where AP = the probability of an accidental launch of a nuclear missile over a period of time; p = the chance of the accidental launch over a 24 hour period; U = the number of United States missiles; S = the number of soviet missiles; and n = the number of days. To show how the equation works, let's say that we want to know the chance of an accident over a one year period. Then n=365 (days); u=2000 (approximately); and we don't know the value of p, but let's assume it is very small like 10 (to the power of -8), or one chance in one hundred million. Inserting these values in to AE we find that the likelihood of an accidental launch in one year is 1.4 percent. In forty years, the likelihood is more than fifty percent."

Lyttle said the United States should have no level of defense. He also believes during a presidential election, his party can get more publicity to its cause.

Enough of this! Put a letter in a mathematical formula and my brain explodes, and my comprehension drops. My chance of not understanding any semi-complicated mathematical formula can best be described as follows:

$$=N(*)b$$

If N =1 and b = 100 and you multiple, then subtract you have the percentage. ZERO!

CHAPTER NINE

HOW THE SPIN WORKS
THE MEDIA CENTER AT THE
VICE PRESIDENTIAL DEBATE

"In public relations, spin is a form of propaganda, achieved through providing an interpretation of an event or campaign to persuade public opinion in favor or against a certain organization or public figure." [1] Nowhere can the spin operation be seen better than at a debate of the Vice President or President of the United States.

Do I have to remind anyone of a few short years ago how funny it was when Republican pundits said repeatedly how qualified Sarah Palin was to be Vice president of the United States? It was funny then and it's funny now. That is what spin is—Sarah Palin is qualified to be Vice President or even President of the United States!

The vice-presidential debate between Joseph Lieberman and Dick Cheney was held in Danville, Kentucky on Thursday, October 5, 2000. It was also held in 2012 in Danville. At noon, Bill Scheyer and I gave a presentation before the Greater Cincinnati Chapter of the American Society of Public Administration about our presidential year. We then drove to Danville. I called Bill Mitchell, a long-time friend who was the Community Development Director in Danville. Mitchell, who was attempting to get us media passes for the debate, told me he had been successful. We arrived in Danville in the mid-afternoon, parked at Millennium Park and took a shuttle into town and immediately found Mitchell. He walked us over to a building where we obtained our media passes. These passes made this trip very successful. We now had access to the entire campus, except for the debate hall. Most importantly, we had full access to the media center and were now in a position to witness the "spin" operation first hand.

We first walked through the media center, held in the campus gym. On the way, Bill Mitchell mentioned how the Presidential Debate Commission explained to the community how to pass ordinances to put protestors in certain areas of the city. The room was set up with tables from front to back with television sets placed in key positions. The room was already a little busy, even though the debate was four hours away. Bill Scheyer and I talked with Jim Nicholson, Chairman of the National Republican Party. We were in the very back of the room and talked briefly about the Republican Convention. Concerning the debates, he said to us, "We've got the momentum back and the activity in Yugoslavia today helps us." It helps show Cheney's foreign policy experience. Nicholson was referring to the breaking news story that Yugoslavian leader Slobodan Milosevic had been overthrown by angry mobs. We shook hands and he said to let him know if there was any way he could help with our presidential year. We then walked to the football practice field about five minutes away. The field was the location of the public speaking area, set aside for organizations to give speeches and set up tables to distribute literature. It was in an inconvenient location, but at least the college set up something for alternative viewpoints. The crowd was very small, perhaps a dozen people. Earlier in the morning, Winona LaDuke, Vice Presidential candidate for the Green Party, spoke. She was already gone and would not be returning. Bill and I spoke to a couple manning the Green Party table, who we met at the Northern Kentucky Green Party meeting earlier in the year. Because of the lack of activity we walked around campus. Two Vice Presidential candidates from third parties would be at the speaker's area later and our goal was to meet them.

Our next stop was to eat. Having passes we could eat all the free food available to the media. A large tent was set up outside the media center for dinner. The three of us were among the first to eat. The food was plentiful and a big piece of carrot cake was my desert. After we ate, they gave us a free commemorative glass inscribed for the debate.

At the speaker's area, we met with Art Olivier, the Vice Presidential candidate of the Libertarian Party. He said he remembered meeting me in Indianapolis. Our conversation with Olivier was very interesting and long. The topics we discussed were varied including his time as Mayor of Belfower, California

and the Libertarian Party in general. Olivier discussed how he
accomplished his goals as mayor. The politics of the city broke
down into honest people verses the "crooks" that had been in
power a long time. His group of "honest" people gradually took
over the city government. He was not specific about this issue
but said people were making money off their positions. He
talked about elections being delayed in the city once. Under
California Law, he said, a council can delay an election vote, I
assume under certain circumstances. He discussed privatization
of the city and that there was little resistance once they gained
control of council. As Mayor, he privatized the city's tree
trimming, crossing guards, street sweeping and building
department and eliminated the city's lighting tax assessment. [2]
Belfower is a city of 77,000 and a suburb of Los Angeles. The
entire city was not privatized and Olivier said the quality of
services improved and they saved money. We asked if he
quantified the results of the privatization of building permits. He
said he "didn't think of it." He mentioned how the community
has been having a lot of housing torn down to make room for
new, more expensive units. When asked if they were destroying
historic property, he said, "No they are old houses of no historical
value."

Olivier talked about growth in the Libertarian Party. It has gone
from 15,000 to 40,000 dues paying members nationwide. Last
evening, he was at a fundraising event for the party. He was
always told, or under the belief, that the Libertarian Party was not
strong in Kentucky. Olivier said, he has "found that not to be
true." They had approximately 50 people at the fundraising event
last evening. We did a lot more talking with Olivier and joked
around some including his speech and when it would happen.
We then went back to the Media Center because Olivier would
not be speaking for a little while. When we came back, we were
told Olivier had already spoken. We told him and he said in a
surprised voice and slightly elevated voice, "You missed it?" He
then joked, "I did it just for you guys." Olivier, as a Libertarian,
talked a lot during the campaign about limited government and
was especially concerned about constitutional rights. He

believed our foreign policy should be based on avoiding alliances that get us into conflicts.

Scheyer and I now wanted to meet Dr. Curtis Fraiser, the Vice Presidential candidate for the Constitution Party. We had been talking with the Constitution Party officials from Kentucky. The preamble of the party says, "we, the members of the Constitution Party, affirm that every citizen is endowed with the inalienable rights to life, liberty, property and pursuit of happiness. It is the function of government to secure these rights by preservation of domestic tranquility, a strong national defense and the promotion of justice for all." They are 100% pro-life, without exception; and want to restore educational freedom, eliminate federal taxes on business and families, strengthen our national defense, protect American independence, restore the right to bear arms, and restore constitutional accountability. Frasier appeared and as we were talking with him, Art Olivier came up and introduced himself. It was exciting, seeing two Vice Presidential candidates up close introduce themselves. I got a great picture of it. Olivier mentioned right away that a Constitution Party official corrected him on one point. Olivier has been saying on the campaign trail that his party is the only one to turn down federal matching funds and he now learned the Constitution Party has done the same. Frasier is an ER Doctor and I had him sign my White House photo and he joked about his handwriting. Fraiser told us his speech will "mostly pick on Republicans because Democrats are easy to figure out." He also said to us that here we are a month before the election and there is a lot of voter apathy. The voters "don't know the issues and then go in and blindly pull the lever." Our conversation with Fraiser was less issue oriented and more like a "friendly chat". Fraiser was a very pleasant guy and meeting him was a goal for the last couple months. We spent time with Fraiser up until he was to speak. He walked on the small stage and began his remarks. The crowd was very small, around 20 people. He had prepared notes that would be great to have. He discussed how the Debate Commission sets forth, as its purpose: "to insure that debates provide the best possible information to viewers and listeners." Fraiser said, "well, pardon me, but this isn't happening! They should call themselves the conspiracy on presidential debates." Fraiser also mentioned the "Democrats and Republicans are going through a carefully crafted script with style but without substance." He said, "Christians and conservatives listen up. The Republicans fly a false flag. Republicans have abandoned principle only to bargain with the Democrats over the details of surrender." "On every key issue, the Republicans and Democrats agree." "Patrick Henry did not say: 'give me more government subsides, take away my guns and give me socialized medicine, or give me death'." He did say: "it is when a people forget God that tyrants forge their chains." The key issues he said are ending abortion as the first action of President Howard Phillips, the Constitution Party presidential candidate, ending the income tax, inheritance tax, capital gains tax, and Social Security tax. "The legitimate functions of government will be funded by a 25% revenue tariff and a few targeted excise taxes."

Frasier said, "the Republicans want you to believe they are doing all they can to end abortion, cut taxes, and stop gun control. But, they fly a false flag." He says they gave us pro-abortion judges, the Brady Bill, and criminalized the practice of medicine through the Dole-Kennedy-Kassabaum Bill. He would get us out of NAFTA and the World Trade Organization and ban homosexuals from the military. He would eliminate funding for Planned Parenthood and the Gay Men's Health Crisis. The crowd seemed to be pretty liberal to me and I was curious how they would react to Fraiser. They gave him polite applause after his remarks. Afterwards, I said to Bill I would like to get the copy of his speech as a souvenir. Thus, in those hopes, I said to Fraiser, I enjoyed his remarks and would like to get a copy of the text sometimes so to tell other people about it. He said, "Here have my copy." He gave me his original speech which had his notes written on it: a nice piece of presidential history.

We then went back to the Libertarian Party table and met Rebecca Novak, a young girl who joined the party because of her opposition to mandatory seat belt laws. Upon leaving the speakers area for the last time, we briefly talked to Olivier again. Before going to the Media Center, Bill and I walked up the street to go to a Cheney pre-debate rally. At the corner of one downtown street, as we waited for the light to change, a car pulled up right in front of us. Former Clinton aide George Stephanopoulos got out and we shook his hand and told him how much we enjoyed his remarks at NKU a couple weeks before. This was the 5000th time we ran into him during the campaign. We didn't have enough time to go to the Cheney event and thus headed back to the Media Center for the debate.

We introduced ourselves to Karen Hughes, George Bush's Communications Director. She said she drove down from Columbus where the Governor's plane was parked. Hughes said "It's great just being off a plane for a while." I asked how she thought the debate would be. "I think he will do a good job," Hughes responded. In the front of the room, each campaign had a help desk set up. I saw Rob Portman, Congressman from Ohio, who played the role of Lieberman in Cheney's debate practices. Also, former Senator Alan Simpson, and Senators Bunning and McConnell were around. Bill Mitchell, Bill Scheyer and I introduced ourselves to Journalist/writer/commentator Robert Novak. We did so because he was not working, just standing around. He was not real nice. Novak, the conservative political commentator died in 2009. A little later, Karen Hughes came back to us and asked, "How are you doing?" About twenty minutes before the debate began. the media center got the live feed from the hall. We had taken seats toward the front, left side of the room, three rows back. Scheyer and I sat together, Mitchell across the aisle. Reporter Pat Crowley described the debate in the newspaper the next day: "It was conversational more than confrontational; a true debate between a couple seasoned politicians who respected one another as they respectfully disagreed. In their only debate of the campaign Thursday night, Vice Presidential candidates Dick Cheney and Joseph Lieberman discussed the issues like two old friends, frequently calling each other by their first names while seated around a table at Centre College. There was none of the jabbing or sniping present in Tuesday's debate between presidential candidates George W. Bush and Al Gore. CNN Anchor Bernard Shaw, who did a good job, moderated the debate. This debate was enjoyable and in sharp contrast to the presidential debates."

As the debate was going on, reporters were busy on their laptop computers. Interestingly, as the candidates spoke, each campaign would constantly feed reporters news releases about what was just said. If, for example, Cheney said something, within five minutes, the Gore Spin operation would have something in writing passed out to each reporter in response. During the course of the debate, I received about 17 of these responses. The Cheney release format had a heading called "setting the record straight" across the top and then sub-headings called "rhetoric" and "facts." The Gore one generally had the heading "Reality Check" and then a specific topic. The sub headings were "rhetoric" and "reality." Here is an example from the Gore Campaign: "Reality Check: RU-486. Rhetoric: Bush-Cheney still failed to answer the RU-486 questions. Reality: Bush-Cheney are contradicting their earlier announced position on RU-486." The Reality section then explained why. This release was distributed within minutes of Cheney's response to the RU-486 question, better known as the abortion pill. Some of the press seemed to read these "spin" papers and others ignored them. The reporter immediately to our left didn't want them. He gestured for them to not give him any.

By the way, around the perimeter of the media center room, were small cubicle areas for television media for broadcasting and interviewing. I have always been fascinated by the spin operation you see on television after debates. It is a very interesting aspect of modern campaigns and I have always wondered what it was like. So far, it had been interesting watching reporters write their stories and observing them in the media center. Parts of it were laid back, reporters just hanging around seemingly relaxed. Other parts included reporters on deadline. Observing people around the media center was very informative. During the debate the reporters were focused on watching. About five minutes before the debate ended, the real spin began. Out of the left side of the room came approximately 20 Democratic "spin" doctors and the Republican ones came out at the same time on the right side. It was literally a parade of these people. Each one had a college student holding a sign in the air indicating who the "spin" person was. They spread across the room wanting to be interviewed.

What struck me the most was the sheer importance of all these spin-doctors. I had the impression before this evening that the spin-doctors were mostly campaign aides. This group of individuals was a who's who of American Politics. It included Senators, Congressmen, Governors, current and former Cabinet Secretaries, campaign aides, etc. It was quite impressive. Bill and I walked around the room getting in the middle of as many press interviews as we could. Karen Hughes said Cheney spoke with authority and his honesty came through. She hoped Lieberman could have convinced Gore to change his positions to his instead of the other way around. She was referring to the positions Lieberman had disagreed with Gore on in the past. Governor Engler of Michigan talked about the military experience of Cheney. Jim Daley, Gore Campaign Chairman, said Lieberman set a positive tone and helped solidify the wise choice Gore made. While listening to Hughes, a guy named Doug Hathaway approached me to be interviewed. This took me by surprise and after stumbling for a second; I fired off a question like "What is your reaction to the debate?" I didn't know who this guy was and thought he might be a Congressman. On election night, I found out he was a Gore Campaign spokesman. He was interviewed a lot on television that evening from Nashville. In response to my question, Hathaway talked about the fact Gore has set aside 300 million in a rainy day fund for social security. This was my first one-on-one interview. Interviews, what a great idea! Why just get in the middle and listen? I should conduct interviews and so I was off.

Donald Rumsfeld, former Secretary of Defense was there supporting Bush. Nobody was interviewing him and he was just walking around waiting for somebody to approach him. Thus, I did. However, I was thinking he was a former Secretary of the Treasury and I introduced myself as being with the *Northern Kentucky ADDvisor*, the name of my work newsletter. What else was I going to say? I had to be from somewhere and I was in fact the newsletter editor. I asked him economic questions. Why was George Bush not addressing the accumulated debt and that a

Democrat, Al Gore was more concerned with debt reduction? "Their programs are based upon revenue projections that many people doubt will be met," commented Rumsfeld. He said projections of revenue are often wrong and "fundamentally dependent on the economy." Cheney is going on estimates by a committee of Congress and Lieberman the Congressional Budget Office. They both have different ways of doing things. "In business and Government, you make budget forecasts. If they are wrong, you adjust. Plans are always evolving." Surprisingly he said Lieberman was "rational and thoughtful on important issues." "Cheney showed a depth of knowledge and what you see is what you get." Rumsfeld was not very concerned with the debt. He said the debt is becoming less of a percentage of total GNP as the economy grows. This interview became even more exciting when President-elect Bush named Rumsfeld as his Secretary of Defense.

Bill and I spent another hour walking around participating in and observing the spin operatives in action. The place was hopping and television interviews were taking place around the perimeter of the room. Print and television media were working the entire room. Obviously, all Democratic spin-doctors thought Lieberman won and same for the Republicans with Cheney. They thought this before the debate ever started. What struck me the most was the large number of spin-doctors. I expected a few key campaign aides. However, their numbers were large and stature great. One Senator, Joe Biden, that we followed a lot, was once a Presidential candidate and of course now Vice President. These people knew what they were going to say before they ever came out. Some reporters didn't even participate in the process, probably because it is so partisan. The next day, in reading the press coverage, I found very few quotes from the powerful spin-doctors. The entire process seemed like something each party did, but really meant nothing. The reporters were not duped by the one-sided spin.

From this experience, I had a much better perspective on how spin operations worked. It was fascinating on one hand and humorous on another. Campaigns followed their scripts and explained how their candidate won. It didn't matter what really happened. Spin was the name of the game. It was all propaganda designed to sway public opinion. While not effective, it was very cool. I was in a room full of the top political pundits and political officials of the time. It was all spin, but it was a political junkie's best dream.

1. *Wikipedia*
2. *Wikipedia, Art Oliver*

CHAPTER TEN

*AL GORE WAS A NO-SHOW
ELECTION DAY 2000*

Election Day 2000 was memorable. I voted at the General Store in Rabbit Hash for George W. Bush for President. My son, Ethan, went into the voting booth with me, and Andrew went in with my wife, Ann.

A little before noon I headed to Nashville and picked up our credentials to visit the Al Gore victory or perhaps condolences party. They were provided by the Tennessee State Democratic Party's Deputy Director Steve Lindsey. He was very confident about the election and said he would be spending the night at headquarters. Despite having his leg in a cast, he offered me a parking spot and walked down to the garage to show how to retrieve the car later.

The next thing to do was to visit the Legislative Plaza at the War Memorial where the Gore festivities would take place. It was too early to go in, so we walked to the State Capitol Building. President James K. Polk, who is an underrated President, is buried on the capitol lawn. We walked around the grave, struck by the fact we did so on the night a new President would be elected. Would it be another Tennessean? Polk moved to Tennessee from North Carolina when he was eleven and died a little more than 150 years ago. Polk had established four goals for his presidency: re-establish the independent treasury system, reduce tariffs, acquire some, or all, of the Oregon Territory, and acquire California and New Mexico from Mexico. He accomplished all of these goals.

On the east side of the Capitol, ten state police officers gathered and were about to begin their evening assignments. Night was falling as we walked up the east steps. Lights were on behind the old side windows of the stately Capitol, giving a warm mellow glow of history. We were feeling good about our country and the history we expected to watch that evening. We felt truly blessed.

After a short walk, we went to the Sheraton Hotel across from the plaza to watch some early election results. The hotel was crowded with Gore supporters and the media. Results started to come in and Kentucky announced for Bush. As states rolled in, it was clear Gore was winning big as the networks announced he had won Michigan, Pennsylvania, and Florida. After getting a sandwich, we entered the plaza. The crowd was jubilant as we entered at Union and Sixth Streets. It appeared to be an easy win for Gore. On the plaza, we settled in for a long evening. Entertainers such as Marilu Henner, Sawyer Brown, Cher, and Morgan Fairchild appeared. Large screens were on each side of the stage for returns. It began to rain and did so all night long. The big issue at this time was how would Tennessee vote? As the rally got underway, it was hard for this crowd to believe Tennessee would go for Bush. The state that started Gore's career 24 years ago did go for Bush. When it did, the crowd was very disappointed and one-person said, "What is wrong with this state?"

In all its glory, the Plaza shined that evening. It was hosting a very historic event with the lighted state Capitol looking overhead. Across the plaza was a very large tower holding media personnel. One could sense the history through the beauty of the surroundings.

Then it all began! A little before 10 p.m., the networks took back their prediction on Florida. I had gone to the bathroom and heard the news on my headphones. The big screen was not giving returns and so I told people in the crowd Florida was back in the "too close to call" column. As word spread, the crowd became concerned. They were scared about what this meant. The rain continued to fall upon the now less jubilant and concerned crowd. Some of the crowd had left because of the rain and the long wait and it was going to be a longer evening than our worst case scenario.

At this point we didn't think security was checking credentials to get in to the closer, restricted section up by the stage. We exited the area where we had entered five hours earlier and, without any problem, walked into the VIP section. Turning our credentials over to hide them, we walked straight to the front and positioned

ourselves about ten to fifteen feet from the podium where we
hoped to hear Gore. We found ourselves on the front steps of
history. The big screens were working now and showing
elections results. They had broken down for a time. All eyes
were on Florida. For a while Bush had a 120,000 Florida vote
lead and Bush was winning the electoral vote but losing the
nationwide popular vote. Nobody was calling for an end to the
Electoral College. Bush's lead dropped to 20,000 and the crowd
was cheering. Each news report had Gore gaining. The crowd
cheered with each report. The Gore supporters had been sure of
victory, sure of loss, and now back in it. Everyone knew the
gravity of Florida. Whoever wins it wins the White House. Then
it came---the networks declared George Bush the winner and the
President-elect. The crowd didn't react. I was surprised by this
lack of reaction and deep down felt they knew he was going to
lose. It seemed like the trend for the last few hours, especially
when the western states started to roll in.

What made this evening truly historic was yet to come. The
crowd was very tired and wet. It was late and we had been on the
Plaza for more than eight hours and Gore had lost. On a loud
speaker, it was announced Gore would arrive in twenty minutes.
He was on his way and we were about eight feet now from where
he would give his concession speech. I watched as the Gore
concession speech was loaded into the TelePrompTer. They
removed the plastic from the microphone that was protecting it
from the rain. Bill was mad that Gore was making the crowd wait
so long. Next to us were three young girls singing but it didn't fit
the somber mood of the crowd.

Florida was then announced again as "too close to call." The
crowd erupted. Was Gore still coming? He never showed up.

In my favorite nuance of history, I watched as the plastic was put
back on the microphone. This simple act was the result of the
greatest change of fortunes in American Presidential history and I
was eight feet way. The crowd booed. Little did I know at the
time the significance of putting the plastic back on the
microphone. We didn't know it, but Gore was no longer going to
speak to the crowd. The networks announced that Campaign
Chairman Bill Daley would address the crowd shortly and the

plastic was removed a second time. The now jubilant crowd was jumping. In an amazing moment, the crowd, started to chant "recount." This was the very first time in this election that recount was uttered publicaly and was an important historical moment. David Von Drehle of *The Washington Post* describes what was happening beneath the Memorial Plaza as Al Gore called George Bush to take back his earlier phone call conceding the election.

> "So it was simple the crowning weirdness on a wild and whiplashed night, one among many bizarre things, when Vice President Gore phoned the Texas Governor's mansion to take back what he'd said about conceding the election to George W. Bush.

> 'Circumstances have changed dramatically since I first called you,' Gore told Bush, according to aides to both men who heard each side of the conversation. News from Florida— very late news—indicated the gap had closed once more in the decisive state and there would be an automatic recount.

> 'The State of Florida is too close to call', Gore said. 'Are you saying what I think you are saying?' Bush asked brusquely, disbelievingly. 'Let me make sure that I understand. You're calling back to retract that concession?'

> 'Don't get snippy about it,' Gore said. 'Let me explain,' he continued. If Bush prevailed in the final count, Gore would immediately offer the Texas Governor his 'full support….But I don't think we should be going out making statements with the State of Florida still in the balance.'

> Bush was incredulous. For an hour, since the networks gave him the victory and Gore called to surrender, Bush had been basking in a

combination of relief and excitement. Now the roller coaster car was plunging again.

Didn't Gore realize that Bush's brother Jeb was standing nearby---Jeb, the Governor of Florida, who had been on the phone to Tallahassee and pecking a computer for hours, monitoring vote patterns that he understood as well as anybody." Jeb's research showed a Bush victory, as George W. now reported to Gore.

'I don't think this is something your brother can take care of,' the vice-president answered coolly. (Another aide remembers it this way: 'with all due respect to your brother, he is not the final arbiter of who wins Florida.' Still another aide recalls that Gore specifically noted that Jeb is the younger brother.)

'Do what you have to do,' Bush said frostily. Gore put down the phone. The suppressed bile of a long campaign bubbled through the 90-second call.

He was surrounded by about 30 of his closest staff members in a bland room beneath Nashville's War Memorial Plaza. Outside, thousands of rain soaked supporters awaited the vice-president. The concession speech was already loaded in the TelePrompTer. Now it was scrapped. Instead, Gore advisor Carter Eskew dashed off remarks for campaign chairman William Daley, who slogged up the wet carpet to the stage to promise a recount.

On that inconclusive note ended the most incredible election night in modern American history. Not even the legendarily close Kennedy-Nixon race of 1960 remained unresolved for so long. Back then, before exit polls and computer voting modeling, the television networks would never have called a

close Florida race for Gore hours prematurely,
then retracted their projection, then given it to
Bush only to take that back, too.

It was a night that began with people worried
about Bush winning the popular vote and Gore
the Electoral College, and ended appearing that
it could produce precisely the opposite result.

A night when campaign professionals felt the
tide running toward Bush, then toward Gore,
then toward Bush and back to Gore---and
where it stops no one yet knows.

A night of sudden reversals and frayed options
of resignation chased by resolve, a high-wire
walk towards the biggest political prize."

Perhaps one of the most historic events I have witnessed occurred
about eight feet from me. Bill Daley, looking distinguished,
walked out without announcement to the podium. He approached
the podium and removed papers from his suit pocket. He said the
Vice President had called Bush to withdraw his concession and
"this campaign is back on." The crowd erupted. After just a
couple minutes, Daley turned and left, making the long walk back
up to the war memorial. The emotion of the crowd was
tremendous. After Dailey, left the crowd dispersed and I went to
get my car and drove home. having been up 29 hours.

What struck me the most about the evening was the dramatic and
constant shift in emotions of the crowd. Also, the beauty of the
Plaza, and the Tennessee Capitol was tremendous. It was an
historic night for the already historic block of downtown
Nashville. If prior to coming to Nashville I had been told Gore
wouldn't make an appearance, the evening would be seen as a
disaster. Instead, the night was more historic by not seeing him.
Upon leaving, the election was close and unclear. Little did I
know the historic events put into motion that evening? The new
President would not be selected for many weeks and the Supreme
Court eventually deciding the issue.

CHAPTER ELEVEN

THE ELECTORAL COLLEGE
A UNIQUELY AMERICAN INSTITUTION

To me, one the worst parts of the 2000 election controversy was when the Gore campaign chairman claimed fraud and Hillary Clinton called for the end of the Electoral College. Although to be fair, Arlen Spector, a Republican, did the same as Clinton. [1] Walter Berns says, "One of the virtues of the Electoral College is, or was, that it regularly produces a President with a clear, immediate, and legitimate claim to the office, in part, because it amplifies the margin of victory in the popular vote." [2] For example, Kennedy won the popular vote by .22 percent, but won the electoral vote 303 to 219. Nixon beat Humphrey 43.42 percent to 42.72 percent; with Wallace getting 13.53 percent. Nixon won the electoral vote 301 to 191 to 46. [3]

In 2000, things changed. The electoral vote came down to Florida and it was not until the Supreme Court ruled in Bush v. Gore six days before the Electoral Colleges were to meet that we knew who won. For the first time since 1888 the President-elect did not win the popular vote.

I expect leaders to lead during a crisis. Calling for the end of the Electoral College during this crisis was irresponsible. It was not Clinton's finest moment. Regardless of how you feel, this was not the right time. The country was in political turmoil and she wanted to amend the constitution during a political crisis. I find that scary.

Our founding fathers established this system as a compromise between those calling for direct election by the people and the Virginia Plan letting Congress choose a President. Of course, that is not the question anymore. The question today is - has it outlived its usefulness? I say "no". It allows smaller states to not be dominated by the larger states during Presidential elections. The Electoral College works and to receive states electoral votes a candidate must win the majority vote. Except in Maine and Wisconsin where it is by legislative district, all the votes go to the candidate winning the majority in each state. New York and California still get 31 percent of the 270 votes needed to win the presidency. It is not like they don't count. However, currently the small states count as well.

Nevertheless, the Electoral College meetings of 2000 were to be historic events and an educational opportunity for many Americans. Until 2000, so many Americans had no idea how the system worked. It needed to be seen firsthand.

THE 2000 ELECTORAL COLLEGE

On December 18, 2000, I attended the meeting of the Kentucky Electoral College. As I walked up the front steps of the magnificent Kentucky Capitol Building on this cold winter day, its beauty stood out. Dedicated in 1910, it is an outstanding building. Upon entering the rotunda, I proceeded to the Kentucky Supreme Court where the Electoral College would be meeting. Arriving early, I wanted to scope out the area and entered the courtroom from the side door. The room in its beautiful elegance was inspiring, dominated by its Honduras mahogany paneling and Old Dutch metal attached to old bronze. There were about five people in the room and they were setting it up. I asked about the meeting and they suggested we put our coats on some seats to save them. They gave me a program, a nice bound copy. For about ten minutes I observed the employees, listening to their conversations, and watching them set up the room. They placed upon the table wooden nameplates for the electors that were created just for this occasion. They were quite nice for a one-time use and a good touch. They discussed one elector who would be seated on the end and whether he would be able to make it up the small ledge to his seat. More on that story later. They set up the podium from which the oath of office would be given to the electors. Outside the window of the Chamber, a television truck stood alone and the bitter cold could be felt through the window pane.

I left the Courtroom to walk around. I observed something going on in the Senate Chambers on the other side of the Capitol. It was a reception given by Senate President David Williams for the electors. Outside the Chamber was food; and Bill Scheyer, of course was with me, - free food - our favorite thing! We entered the reception through the Senate doors. We stood in the back of the room for a while and we talked briefly with some local officials from our area of the state. President Williams began to speak and so we walked to the front of the room and stood on the right side. The electors who were standing in the front of the Chamber were each introduced. Six of the eight were there at this point in time and the other two came a few minutes later. Congressmen Ron Lewis and Ernie Fletcher spoke. Williams called him "Landslide Ernie," because of his recent easy re-election to Congress. David Armstrong, the Mayor of Louisville, gave a good speech. Both he and Fletcher, the future Governor, talked about the history of the occasion and the important constitutional duties of the electors. It was like a pep talk. This event was a Republican Party event. It was a partisan affair, which was fine. It was very nice to see a fun reception celebrating the victory of a candidate and honoring members of the Kentucky Electoral College. The crowd was jubilant and numbered approximately 75-100. Often, you heard people comment on the historical significance of the day. All day, people were keenly aware of the history they were experiencing, but most had never attended a College meeting before.

We arrived back in the Supreme Court Chamber around 10:15 a.m. We grabbed our jackets and moved to the second row bench on the right side of the Chamber. As we waited, television crews set up their cameras right in front of people. They, in their typical fashion, were rude and inconsiderate. This meeting of the College would be run by John Y. Brown, III. Brown was elected Secretary of State in 1996 and served until 2004. He is the son of former Governor John Y. Brown, and was an unsuccessful candidate for Lieutenant Governor when he ran with speaker of the House Jody Richards. They lost in the primary election.

At 11:30 a.m. the Secretary of State began the meeting and did so in a very strange manner. He yelled very loudly into the microphone, "hey" to get the crowd's attention. Very strange! He introduced the Kentucky State University Concert Choir under the direction of Dr. Carl Brown. Brown, in introducing them, explained they had to leave after their performance. Then Brown said he wanted to let us know it's not a "protest or anything." This was not an appropriate comment and apparently assumed because the choir was all African American, they were against Bush. He just didn't need to say something so stupid. The choir sang a beautiful rendition of "America" and received a standing ovation. During the song, a reporter talked loud on his cell phone and disturbed the crowd. He continued to talk during the next few minutes of the meeting as well. There was also the Pledge of Allegiance, led by State Board of Elections member, Charles W. Buchanan. Brown said this meeting is "a lot bigger event than in 1996." The crowd gave a large cheer. He called this a time-honored event for over 200 years. A chosen few citizens participate. He said, "I congratulate you on your selection." This, Brown said, is the same system put into place over 200 years ago as the most appropriate, equitable way of selecting the President and Vice President.

Brown then conducted the roll call of electors. Kentucky Supreme Court Chief Justice Joseph E. Lambert was introduced. Lambert, a former staff member of U.S. Senator John Sherman Cooper, became Chief Justice just a couple years before this meeting of the Electoral College. It was his first time administering the oath. He said this has served as the room for the highest court for 100 years. Many momentous events have occurred. Not until today has there been a decision so pivotal to the election of a President and Vice President. Electors are here today to select a President. The Electoral College is obscure but not today. Judge Lambert said, "The eyes of the nation are on these electors." The Judge then administered the oath of office to the eight electors. William Farish, elector from the Sixth District, was elected Permanent Chair. He announced that Dean Johnson resigned because he held an elected county position, which disqualifies him from serving. The State Director, Ellen

Williams, of the Republican Party, appointed a replacement. The replacement was Douglas Reece and Farish said the electors need to ratify this appointment. John Y. Brown then interjected that before they do this, they should first select a Secretary. Brown said they should do this so as to "not mess up" anything. Elector Connie Hayes, from the Third District, and the only woman, was elected Secretary. Farish then re-read his motion to ratify Reece as an elector, which passed unanimously. Reece was then sworn in again by the Chief Justice.

Senate President David Williams then gave welcome remarks and mentioned the division that exists in the country but said the election proved the system worked as "we reaffirm we are a union of states." Secretary of State Brown then passed out ballots to the electors. There were many copies and the electors spent the next fifteen minutes voting and signing the ballots. Brown jokingly announced "so far it's looking good for Bush." The room was basically quiet during the time the ballots were being signed. People were appreciating watching the system being implemented. It was an historic occasion and Bill and I watched closely. The electors quietly went about their job without much emotion as all the eyes of the room were upon them. Cameras clicked as people took pictures. At the conclusion, Brown collected the ballots and began counting them. In a very funny moment, he counted a few and then looked puzzled about one ballot. He then removed his glasses and held it up to the light. The crowd roared with laughter and applause. This, of course, was a takeoff on the recount vote in Florida that lasted over a month. One of the most enduring visuals of the recounts and legal challenges was a judge holding ballots in the air to determine if the hole was punched through. Brown then announced the results of the election: eight votes for Bush and eight for Cheney. He then signed the ballots. Immediately upon adjournment, Bill and I walked straight up to the front of the room by the electors. We started on the left side of their table and worked our way toward the right. We talked with each elector and shook his or her hand and obtained their autographs on my program. The electors names were as follows: G. Richard Noss, Jr. (State at Large), Michael A. Shea (State at Large), Larry

Joe Walden (First District), George S. Beard, (Second District), Connie S. Hayes (Third District), Robert B. Fearing (Fourth District), A. Douglas Reece (Fifth District), and William S. Farish, Jr. (Sixth District). Without exception, each was excited to be an elector during this historic election and appreciated its significance. They took the job seriously. We had our picture taken with Farish because he was Chair of the Electors. I asked Reece how long ago had he found out he would be an elector. He said two weeks and it was prearranged that he would be sworn in twice. Each elector was very nice and was basking in the spotlight and fame they had on this one special day.

Watching these individuals enthusiastically participate in the process was inspiring. While the Electoral College was facing some criticism, this meeting was a completely positive experience, which helped show firsthand how brilliant our founding fathers were. I have attended each meeting of The Kentucky Electoral College since 2000, including 2008 when the first African American President was elected, although the Kentucky votes went to McCain. The year 2008 was the first time Kentucky picked the loser since 1960. The same thing happened in 2012, as Kentucky Electors went with Romney.

Perhaps the beauty and wisdom of the Electoral College can be seen in its simplicity. I learned in 2000 how simple the meeting was, held at the same time in state Capitals across the country. It was just common folks meeting to elect the President of the United States. It was, at its core, a simple meeting with some pomp and ceremony added for flavor and to accentuate the historical significance of the event. One great example of the beauty of the College was elector Robert Fearing.

Fearing was seventy years old and had a stroke two weeks before the meeting. The day before, he checked himself out of the hospital so he could attend this meeting of the Electoral College. I asked the lady who was helping him around if he could sign my program and she said he has been signing his name a lot and would be glad to. Fearing was the person, when they were setting up the room, that staff wondered would he be able to make it over the small step to sit behind the table with the other electors. He did make it. Fearing was in his wheelchair the entire time. He said in the paper the next day "this is something very special" and "if there was any way possible, I was going to be here." This man was truly inspiring and a pleasure to meet.

Secretary Brown spoke poorly and could hardly be heard during this meeting. He seemed young and inexperienced although he had been Secretary of State for four years. As we waited to talk with Brown, he said to someone that for the first time in his life, the Congress, Senate, and Presidency are all controlled by Republicans. Perhaps, he said, " I should get my resume together." I asked Brown, because he is the Chief Elections Officer for the State, what he thinks about ballot access issues related to third parties. He answered something about the Supreme Court and the 15% requirement to get in the debates. He mentioned how Ross Perot, because he was in the debate a few years ago, brought the issue of the budget deficit to the forefront. I restated my question and he talked about New Jersey having a 750,000 signature requirement for third parties. There is no way it is that large. He didn't seem to understand the issue or to speak eloquently on it. I was very surprised given his position. We asked him what physically happens to the ballots now that they are signed. He said one goes to the National Archives and one to the Senate where, he said, Vice President Gore would "open them on the 5th or 6th." The other copies go somewhere else. He didn't know where. We asked how the official one would get to the Senate. He said through "certified mail." Makes sense! We chuckled, thinking it would be something more official. We all also laughed again about his holding the ballot up to the light to look at it. He liked our feedback. Our conversation with Brown was very pleasant and special, especially given the historic context in which it took place. We had our picture taken with him and I had him sign my program.

I saw a piece of paper on the podium and took it. It was Senator Williams notes from his speech. We then walked up to the Office of the Chief Justice on the other side of the Capitol. He was not in, but his secretary let us go into his office to look around. She then joined us. She had been working for the Chief Justice for twenty-five years, back to when he first started out as a lawyer. "He is a real family man," she said. Indeed, we noticed his wife's picture under the glass on his desk. It was unique in that the picture was on the side of the desk where guests would sit (opposite the Chief Justice) and it was facing front. The Chief Justice was at lunch and would be back in twenty minutes. His secretary said we could wait if we wanted. We took a walk, stopping at the chapel down the hall. After he returned, we had a brief conversation. We talked about the historic nature of this meeting of the Electoral College. Judge Lambert said he recognized the history of today's event and thus brought his two sons along. He thoroughly enjoyed presiding over the meeting and would remember it all his life.

THE 2008 KENTUCKY ELECTORAL COLLEGE MEETING

December 15, 2008 was my third straight time to attend a meeting of the College. I mention it, specifically, because on this date Barak Obama, the first African American, was elected as President of the United States. There was nothing particularly exciting about this meeting. This was in part because it was Republican electors because McCain won Kentucky in the Presidential election. However, Obama won the presidency. The Capitol Building was not very busy, although there were around fifty people in the rotunda for some kind of program for law enforcement personnel. Twenty-one people were in the audience at the Electoral College, not counting the press. This was the smallest crowd of the four Electoral College meetings I have attended.

I went to the Supreme Court Chamber around 11:20 a.m. and sat and waited. The crowd started to come in about ten minutes later. Upon arriving there were only a handful of people. Secretary of State Trey Grayson arrived a couple minutes prior to the program beginning. The week before, Trey and I talked at the Urban Active Gym in Florence about the Electoral College meeting. He said that earlier in the day he had just sent to D.C. the certification of the election of Senator Mitch McConnell, who won in a close election over Bruce Lunsford. He was looking forward to his first meeting of the Electoral College.

Electors voted by signing ballots and then signing certifications. The signing process took around 25 minutes which occupied, by far, most of the time the meeting actually took place. This meeting was pretty straight forward and not very exciting. I am glad I attended, especially since the election was so historic with the election of the first African American President. Needless to say, the Electors voted 8-0 for McCain and separately 8-0 for Sarah Palin.

So what did I learn about the Electoral College? I was most impressed by the simplicity of the whole thing, including the voting. Call me an optimist, or a defender of our system, I will not apologize. Where Hillary Clinton saw a constitution that no longer worked and needed to be changed in the midst of a crisis; I saw the beauty of it all. Mostly, I was proud of the system that could go through this crisis and do so nonviolently and governed by the rule of law.

Simple, but in a way inspiring, this uniquely American institution, created by our founding fathers, was little more than a meeting similar to any taking place in board rooms across America. The electors were regular people fulfilling a constitutional duty. Only a few people go to witness this, but that doesn't matter. It barely makes the news the next day. It is a formality evidenced by witnessing one. My son, Ethan, called the 2012 meeting of the Electoral College "boring." Maybe so, but seeing it first-hand helps to understand what the founders saw in creating this odd process upon which the election of the President of the United States stands.

1.   *Democracy and the Constitution, Walter Berns, The AEI Press, 2006.*

2.   *Democracy and the Constitution, Walter Berns, The AEI Press, 2006*

Bob on Capitol grounds following
the first inauguration of President Clinton

Bob and Bill Scheyer with Republican Party Chairman, Jim Nicholson,
following the 2000 inauguration of President George W. Bush

Bob and his son, Ethan, at the inauguration of the first
African American President, Barack Obama

George W. Bush on the campaign trail, in Iowa, in 2000

At Bob and Edith's; Bob's favorite diner in America

Bob and Bill Scheyer with President Bush's Treasury Secretary Designee, Paul O'Neill, following his confirmation hearing

At the White House on the last day of the Clinton Presidency

Senator Robert Byrd's caisson passes on its way to the West Virginia Capitol

CHAPTER TWELVE
PRESIDENTIAL INAUGURATIONS

According to Paul F. Boller, Jr., George Washington's inauguration as the first President of the United States on April 30, 1789, was a momentous event. In a world ruled largely by Kings, queens, czars, emperors, shoguns, and sultans, the American people were trying something different: a representative government based on the freely given consent of the governed. There was no certainty of success." [1]

Nothing in my mind compares to the historic feel and experience of a Presidential inauguration. It is the cream da la crème of history. When asked about the first president being the most important, George Washington said, "It is the second one." He was referring to the first transfer of power from him to Adams. The peaceful transfer of power from one president to another is the greatest experience of history watching. While I have witnessed much history, inaugurations are my favorite. It is best to experience inaugurations by investing an entire week in Washington D.C. The capital city is experiencing the end of a presidency and the beginning of a new one. Our history is, and will forever be, defined by the individual presidencies that start with an inauguration. Perhaps one of the greatest events in American history occurred in 1797. John Adams became the second President of the United States. The first peaceful transfer of power happened between the ever popular Washington and Adams. The nation wept as the great Washington left public service for good. In every inauguration since, the nation successfully passed power peacefully from one president to another. Two inaugurations saw massive protests. One was Nixon's second and one was the first inauguration of George W. Bush.

Having attended the two previous inaugurations of Bill Clinton, I knew what to expect. However, given the controversial manner in which George W Bush was elected, I was in for a surprise.

In 2000, I started out at the Iowa Caucuses and over the year, traveled approximately 15,000 miles following the campaign and the history of the first presidential election of the new century. My goal was to go from Iowa to the Inauguration.

GEORGE W. BUSH

The wakeup call was early on Inauguration Day. Our standing room section was right up front and on the South side. The sidewalks were crowded because Independence Avenue had been cordoned off. We made it through security pretty quickly and found a standing room spot in the first row, against the section rope. Our angle was great for the swearing-in. We were about seventy-five yards away from the inaugural stand, the closest I have ever been for an Inauguration. We were behind a large press stand but the gaps were so large we could see really well.

We passed the time talking, reading, and observing people. Mayor Rudolph Guiliani from New York City walked in front of us by about 50 feet and the entrance to the premium seats was right in front of us. I mention this because the mayor of the country's largest city would be propelled into a tragic role following the 9/11 terrorist attacks nine month later. He would shine and become a national hero. Approximately 45 minutes before the ceremony, the U.S. House of Representatives were introduced (as a whole). Others were introduced: former Vice President Dan Quayle, former Presidents Jimmy Carter and George H.W. Bush and their wives, and current President Bill Clinton and First Lady Hillary Clinton. Upon Clinton's introduction, there were boos to be heard in the crowd. This was pathetic. Here we are at an Inauguration and the crowd boos the current President of the United States. Al Gore received a similar, but less noisy, boo. Also, one observation I had, was the crowd at this Inauguration was a lot less racially diverse than the last two.

One of the great moments of the day was when Senator Mitch McConnell came up to the podium to begin the swearing-in ceremony. McConnell and his wife were introduced to the crowd earlier. McConnell introduced the son of the Reverend Billy

Graham, who gave the invocation and the DuPont Manual High School/Youth Performing Arts School Choir from Louisville, Kentucky followed him. McConnell then introduced Chief Justice William Rehnquist to administer the Vice Presidential Oath of Office. At the end, the Chief Justice said one of my favorite lines, "Congratulations Mr. Vice President." I had a great line of sight for the swearing-in. The crowd cheered and a few minutes later Staff Sergeant Alec T. Maly of the United States Army Band sang a medley of American songs.

Then it was the President's turn and the historic moment was upon us. McConnell re-introduced the Chief Justice to administer the Presidential Oath of Office. I was excited and the crowd cheered and the oath was given. "Congratulations Mr. President," said Rehnquist. Just like that, the country had a new President. Abraham Lincoln said, "It is but ordinary charity to attribute the fact that in so attaching himself to the party which his judgment prefers, the citizen believes he thereby promotes the best interests of the whole country, and when an election is passed, it is altogether befitting a free people that, until the next election, they should be as one people." The country starts anew. As Bush 41 said in his opening inaugural line, "This peaceful transfer of authority is rare in history, yet common in our country. With a simple oath, we affirm old traditions, and make new beginnings." McConnell, as the first person ever, introduced "President George W. Bush". That was an historic moment. The new President thanked Clinton for his service and said of Al Gore, "I thank Vice President Gore for a contest conducted with spirit, and ended with grace".

Hearing Bush's inaugural speech, it was all right, but nothing special. Later, after reading it, I liked it much more. It reads well and is probably a little better than average. It's just Bush is not a great speaker. After the address, the invocation was given and mentioned Jesus, a couple times. This became controversial because of the millions of Americans who do not believe in Jesus, even though they believe in God. It seemed to many, to be inconsistent with Bush's message of inclusion. SSGT Maly sang the National Anthem and the ceremony was over.

Bill and I immediately made our way to the now unsecured area up front. Most people simply leave the grounds when the ceremony is over. Not us! We made our way to the area right in front of the inaugural stand and we did this at both of Clinton's Inaugurations. It is neat to stand in such a historic location immediately after the event. We made it up so fast this time that we enjoyed the Marine band for a few minutes. They were still playing right in front of the Inaugural stand. I always go up and touch the stand and had to wait this time because the band was still playing. In the meantime, Jim Nicholson, Chairman of the National Republican Committee was standing nearby. I observed Nicholson talking to some "hotshot" who said he couldn't clap for Bill Clinton when he was introduced. Nicholson, to my pleasure, didn't respond. Bill and I talked with him for a couple minutes and discussed seeing him at the Vice Presidential debate in Danville. Nicholson would serve in the Bush Administration as Secretary of Veterans Affairs for a short time. I then went up front where the band was breaking down their equipment and stepped up on their platform and walked up to the inaugural stand and touched it. Looking up at the Presidential seal, I was inspired by its beauty and importance. A half hour earlier, the newly sworn in President gave his acceptance speech a few feet above this now historic artifact. We were wet. It had been raining on and off all day.

Bill and I worked our way up Pennsylvania Avenue to get to our reserved seats for the Inaugural Parade. Every Inaugural parade has protestors. The last two had handfuls of protestors scattered throughout. This time, they were everywhere. It is said the protests at this year's parade were the biggest since Nixon's second Inauguration in 1973, mostly because of the Vietnam War.

Our seats were on the North side of Pennsylvania Avenue. We had to get across, which was no easy feat. We were at the southeast corner of Third Street and Constitution Avenue, trying to get to the other side. We were stopped because the bomb squad was inspecting a "suspicious package." Also, military personnel needed to walk down the sides of the street. The all clear was given and we crossed and made our way down the last little section of Constitution to Pennsylvania. Our seats, for which we paid $50.00, were on Pennsylvania, between 13th and 15th Streets. After a long crowded walk, we made it to our area, which was on Freedom Plaza and protesters were everywhere. We quickly discovered that Freedom Plaza was ground zero for the protesters. We were right in the thick of things and that was perfect to us. The parade was an hour away and we made our way to our seats in a tall bleacher. The bleacher next to us had been taken over and was full of protesters. They overpowered the Girl Scouts volunteers who were tearing tickets. The sidewalk around Freedom Plaza was packed with protesters and one had a loud bullhorn in which he never stopped talking. Often he used profanity including the F-word.

Generally speaking, the protesters called Bush a racist and a murderer. They were strongly opposed to the death penalty and there were anarchists among the protesters. Many protesters were there to "denounce his ascension to power," according to the *Washington Post*. Directly across from our seat was the reviewing stand of the Mayor of Washington. New York Mayor Rudolph Giuliani was in the reviewing stand and needless to say, the protesters gave him a hard time. They shouted "Amadu", the name of an individual shot by the New York Police in a recent controversial case of excessive police force. The Post described the Freedom Plaza scene as follows: "thousands of protesters converged on Freedom Plaza, at 13th Street and Pennsylvania Avenue, to demonstrate against the Bush presidency and his position on a number of issues. In a constant cacophony that boomed through downtown's concrete canyons, some used bullhorns to denounce Bush while others beat plastic buckets with drumsticks to give the gathering a kind of energy and momentum."

The demonstrator's concerns were myriad, but a common theme was the belief that Bush was unfairly given the presidency in a recount process that was rigged. "Bush was selected by big corporations and special interests and not elected by the people. And as a working-class person, I feel we have to vigorously fight against this man," said Oscar Ovalles, 40, a truck driver from Queens, N.Y. "The protesters' presence annoyed many in the shivering crowd." I love a good protest and Bill and I regularly seek them out at historic events. This was clearly one of the biggest I have seen and it had the potential to explode. Protesters of less than ten people didn't need a permit in Washington on Inauguration day. Freedom Plaza was a convergent point for many small groups. I appreciate people who care about issues and make their voice heard and we have had many great memories in protests. However, I will say this group was obnoxious and unconcerned about others rights. They would make generalizations about people or groups of people, thus showing a tremendous level of intolerance and ignorance. They took over a section in which people paid $50.00 to sit.

After a while, the Bush supporters' first, and only overt act of defiance, was to shout his name –"Bush, Bush, Bush." This was after a good hour of listening to the bullhorn, cuss words, and protests. The protesters response was to yell names at the group and make some not so kind gestures. Don't ever give me the pretentious argument that tolerance only exists on the left side of the political spectrum. Eventually, the parade started its way up the Avenue. The first thing was the presidential Motorcade. Not far from us, the motorcade stopped. We saw a swarm of security people get around the presidents car and I had never seen such a show of security. They were preparing to go by our area and it was an intense situation. The cars came past and President Bush could be seen through his car window. Cheney then followed, and could also be seen. They both sat in their cars on our side. The crowd response was a mixture of cheers, jeers, and gestures. The crowd was loud and being in the thick of things was great. We were seeing some great history and these protests definitely defined the parade. To my surprise, most people I talked with back home had no idea as to the level of protesters that were at the parade. After the motorcade passed, the crowd dispersed a lot. The parade started to make its way toward Freedom Plaza. I went over to the edge of my bleacher section to watch, as many of the protesters were leaving. One lady from our section, showing the same narrow-minded attitude as the protesters, yelled, "get a job." A few yelled back, "I have one" or "I have one, thank you." One guy interviewed me for a documentary he was doing on the Florida election and then we watched the parade for a while. Later, leaving our seats, Bill and I started to walk in the direction of the parade, in order to watch it a lot quicker. Everywhere were protesters, who were still walking around but the protesters seemed peaceful. A few times along the route we stopped to watch the parade more closely. One place we paused was at the Navy Memorial on Pennsylvania. Earlier, fifty police officers charged the crowd at the Memorial, as a few people climbed it via the ship mast, replacing the Navy flags with a black and red anarchist flag. The only pro Bush protesters we saw were a group of young kids against abortion. During our walk, my camera malfunctioned and I lost all my parade and protest photos. As we reached the starting point, the last parade entry began their march. Just like last Clinton inauguration, as we got to the starting point, the last entry began. It was funny how that timing was perfect two inaugurations in a row. Our day was now almost over and in it we had been witness to the great traditions, philosophy, and unfortunately, the divisiveness, and separations that define America.

After finishing with the parade, Bill and I fulfilled another tradition. Walking up to Capitol Hill, to the scene of the Inauguration five hours earlier was something emotional to me. This is one of my favorite things to do. At the entrances there was one not blocked. With little effort we made our way all the way up to the front of the seated area that was near where we stood for the Inauguration. There were a few dozen workers moving their equipment. Daylight was gone and night was almost there. It was a little dark and a little light. To be at this spot where so many people observed such a truly historic event, and it's now empty, provided a unique perspective and set of emotions. I love to witness and really "feel" history. By coming back to a spot like this, under these circumstances, you could "feel" it. The stand was still there, but the Presidential Seal was gone. Because of the rain, the grounds were very muddy. The spot where we watched the Inauguration was but an empty field of grass. A lone guard stood at the base of a set of stairs leading to the Inaugural stand. A few office lights shined brightly from the magnificent Capitol. As I stood there looking out on the empty grounds and the sea of chairs, it was neither day nor evening. My mood was also in between. I was struck by the excitement of a bright new beginning for the country and experiencing the melancholy of standing on this historic, but now lonely ground, hours after it launched a new chapter in American History.

And I also thought............ I had made it from Iowa to Inauguration!

OBAMA'S INAUGURATIONS

Inauguration Day, January 20, 2009

What a historic day this will be! Our group of ten people, including my son Ethan, was up and at the nearby bus stop at 5:30 a.m. The bus was not crowded and we took it the one mile to Pentagon Station. This started four and a half hours of misery. The subway is always crowded on inauguration morning and usually, the platforms are jam packed. They were less crowded than normal, however, on the trains, we were packed tight and it took us two hours to get to the Capitol South subway stop, a trip of normally 15 minutes. At almost every stop, and many places in between, the train would pause for backups and each backup lasted around 15 minutes. It was not fun! Eventually we got off the subway train and exited the station but things got much worse.

Let me start by saying there were no more tickets issued for this inauguration than the others I have attended. We had good standing room tickets in the middle section directly behind the seats. Many people that had tickets didn't get in the Inauguration. I can't imagine spending all the money, time and emotion coming to the Inauguration and not getting in, but that is what happened to many. It happened because of what was the worst plan for crowd control I have ever seen. Granted, there were many more people coming to this inauguration, but most of them would be on the Mall. The ticketed area was by the Capitol, and again the same number as previous, recent inaugurations. This always worked fine. This year they merged the lines for the different tickets by having different colors going to the same area. Usually, the colors are separated so there are less people in an area. This year everyone was together creating large problems and signage for ticket lines was very poor. No barricades to separate the lines were set up; and no personnel to guide the lines to keep them together were present. There was no police presence near the lines. Instead of having Mall people and ticketed people separated, they had people with no tickets going through this area. If an official could be found to ask a question, conflicting explanations were given.

The result of all this was a sea of people all merged into one area with no information. People were standing on top of each other and new people arriving and simply merging or going ahead of those that had been waiting for hours. After a couple hours in line, we had to leave this line or not get in. I had my doubts we would get in so we left and followed our line for a couple hundred yards and merged back in under an area that led to a fenced in section. In the area we were in now, we were jam packed and could only move by duck walking. After maybe an hour and a half, we made it through security and ran to the Capitol lawn and were at the Inauguration by about 11:00 a.m., approximately 5 ½ hours after arriving at the bus stop near our hotel.

We were excited and relieved to be in! We had made it and Ethan and I knew the crowd and wait was well worth it. It is just sad that so many didn't get in. Following the crowd rules meant you didn't get in.

We were lined up perfectly in front of the Inaugural Stand and the entire Capitol building stood out ready for a new chapter in American history. It was cold, but probably not as bad as previous days. However, because of standing around so much, it felt colder. We watched as dignitaries were introduced. Most of the seats behind the podium were already filled. By the end of the day, we saw five Presidents in person: HW Bush, Clinton, Carter, W. Bush, and Obama; four Vice Presidents: HW Bush, Quayle, Gore, and Mondale. I can't remember if I saw Cheney because he was in a wheelchair and I don't think I ever laid eyes on him.

Ethan was in awe being at this historic point in time. I don't remember ever being asked when the first African American president would be elected. Colin Powell perhaps could have achieved this honor had he run in 2000. Not in my lifetime probably would have been my answer. I voted for Obama even though his record indicated he is an extreme leftist as defined by the American political spectrum. Bush and the Republicans and the Democratic Congress have done nothing to solve problems.

The Bush Administration had only about ½ hour to go as Ethan and I continued to watch. We watched as Joe Biden took the Oath of Office. Upon "Congratulations, Mr. Vice President" the crowd cheered. On the lawn there were different levels of reactions as President Bush received light applause; showing respect for our President and to the Presidency. I told Ethan he should always respect both, as we applauded President Bush.

Singer Aretha Franklin sang a terrible rendition of America the Beautiful.

Chief Justice Roberts was introduced to administer his first Oath of Office. As the new and young Chief Justice, this should be the first in a long list of Presidents he will swear in. The moment was historic. Cameras snapped, the quiet crowd was focused on the inaugural stand. The oath was administered and Obama was the 44th President of the United States. A 21-gun salute sounded loudly in the distance, the crowd erupted and the greatness of America was on full display. Ethan and I both felt the enormity of the moment.

The crowd was made up of many more African Americans than I have ever seen at an Inauguration. Although, I could never personally feel the moment in the same way they did, I felt so good about America. Inaugurations do that because they are the greatest demonstration of what makes America special. But this time it was different. Looking at the Capitol Building, built in part by the hands of slaves, we just swore in our first African American President.

Our nation was founded on the greatest of principles and political thought in human history. As a nation, we have struggled to fully implement these principles. Much like Jefferson, the man who wrote them on parchment, he didn't live the magnificent words, and we as a country have often ignored them. Today, however, I couldn't help but believe we made tremendous strides toward "a more perfect union."

After the ceremony, Ethan and I were able to climb over some barricades and make our way to the Inaugural stand. We touched the stand on which Obama took the oath an hour earlier. We had our pictures taken and we looked down the Mall at the dispersing crowd.

After the stand/podium visit, we saw General Colin Powell waiting to be interviewed by CNN. We then headed over to Constitution Avenue by the Capitol and near the Robert Taft Memorial. President Obama was having lunch in Statuary Hall, a room we had visited on Friday. We wanted to watch the new President's limo go by.

As tradition dictates, President Bush and Laura climbed into a helicopter on the east side of the Capitol. Soon the former President's helicopter appeared behind the Capitol and flew down the Mall. It flew slowly as Ethan and I watched this very historic moment. Former President Bush was having his final flight around the Capitol. Looking at both the helicopter and the Capitol in the same view was especially sentimental as the former President flew off into history. As they did, a father and son watched.

The wait for Obama's limo should have been a lot less than it was. However, during lunch, Senator Ted Kennedy, suffering at the time from brain cancer, had a seizure. He was rushed to a hospital. Robert Byrd, sitting at the same table had to be taken to his office after suffering from, I believe, exhaustion. Ironically, as we were leaving the Capitol grounds, the jumbotron showed the scene inside Statuary Hall including Ted Kennedy at his table.

After a two hour wait the Military portion of the parade started. Honor Guards had lined the route for as long as we had been waiting and we were frozen from standing in the cold so long. This little section of Constitution Avenue is right before its intersection with Pennsylvania Ave. The parade started with the military marching, followed by the new President.

The President's limo came into view and was about 20 feet in front of us. The new President was on our side of the car and was clearly visible. He smiled and waved right at us. It could not have been a better view and again, it was well worth the wait.

We walked over to Union Station and it was packed, the subway line extending from the top of the elevators all the way out toward the street. Ethan and I were not trying to get a subway. We were just exploring, witnessing the crowded city celebrating the new President. We walked down to Chinatown and ate lunch. This was our third time to eat in Chinatown on this trip. The streets were very crowded. Ethan had more sushi and the hot tea was terrific.

The Inauguration of Barack Obama certainly was a major historic event for the United States – the first African American President. This clearly was a tremendous accomplishment as America made another step toward living the true meaning of our Constitution and core beliefs. This step, or rather leap, is incredible, coming only a little more than 40 years after the adoption of the Civil Rights Laws of the 1960's.

There are many observations about this Inauguration. First, I was surprised how President Lyndon Johnson was regarded during this historic moment. He, more than any President, made this day possible. Lincoln was the President that Obama highlighted during his Inauguration speech and in the months since his election. Johnson was ignored at the same time his impact was played out on a worldwide stage. Think of all of Johnson's policies that helped make this day possible. Paramount of them must be the Civil Rights Act of 1964. The day just seemed like the fulfillment of Johnson's legacy and no one noticed.

Most of the people coming from out of town for the inauguration started arriving on the weekend. Prior to that time, DC seemed pretty normal and clearly the amount of African Americans coming to an Inauguration was at an all-time high. This was good to see. How could a white American possibly feel the emotions African Americans were having at this moment in time.

Especially given where they were just 40 years ago; and with our country's terrible treatment cf black citizens throughout history. As the weekend went on, the numbers far exceeded any other inauguration. With that said, the same can be said of whites also. By inauguration day, the Mall was packed from one end to the other – whites and blacks watching the inauguration in numbers greater than any in history. It was a unique and amazing sight to look down the Mall at the mass of humanity.

It was amazing how very poorly planned the crowd control was on Inauguration Day. There was no excuse. I know the crowd was in record numbers, but it was sheer incompetence how it was handled. In terms of the ticketed area, nothing had changed from previous inaugurations. The Senate, Capitol Police, Secret Service, and the DC Police all ignored previous experiences of what worked and implemented a system that was nothing short of stupid. Senator Dianne Feinstein of California was in charge and I guess deserves the blame, although as a Senator she will never accept it. There was little common sense applied to the planning.

I was very surprised how few public events were held for average citizens. The two Clinton and Bush inaugurations I attended had a large amount of free public events for the average citizen. Obama was mostly ticketed and not for the general public. The only event in which you didn't need a ticket was the concert on the Mall on Sunday. I have always been able to purchase tickets to sit at the Inaugural Parade, but they were always made available to the general public. This time, they were not made available to regular citizens – you had to know somebody. In the past it was great to watch fireworks over the Capitol city on the eve of the Inauguration. Not this time. Contrary to what you might think, the lead up to the Inauguration of Obama was not open to the general public. Obama possess himself as a champion of the common people but put on an inauguration for fat cats.

I voted for George Bush twice but was very glad to see him go. George W. Bush very possibly ended his Presidency as one of the worst two-term presidents in the history. However that is impossible to know. History, especially after several decades is a better judge of a presidency. In essence, it is impossible to tell

how good a president was until years later. I will admit that
history may be a little kinder to him, because of the Iraq War.
The War may prove tremendous in 20 years, possibly realigning
the politics of the Middle East. Dick Cheney was a horrendous
Vice President in my opinion, while at the same time having a
tremendous impact on the Presidency he served. I am not sure
any VP had such an impact. Unfortunately, it was mostly
negative. His hard right, no compromise approach conflicted
with Bush's natural tendencies and kept Bush from being the
President he might have been. Why, because Bush at his core is
a person open to working with both parties and compromising to
move the country forward. Cheney made him a hard liner.

As President Bush's helicopter flew over the capitol one last
time, you could see right before your eyes, the end of a
presidential era, and a respectful, but thankful goodbye.

The best part of the inauguration week was having Ethan, my
son, with me. I had a tremendous time with him and felt like I
had experienced one of the great moments of my life. We shared
a great piece of American history together. Walking the streets
of Washington for six days around this inauguration brought us
even closer together as we discussed and witnessed this point in
time in American history. Ethan saw for the first time most of
the memorials and monuments of the city. Years from now, he
will return, probably without me. The monuments will not have
changed. He will be older and I am sure he will look back fondly
at the great history we shared.

OBAMA TWO

"Hope" didn't pan out the way we all wanted. I voted for
Romney during Obama's second election but still went to the
inauguration of in 2013. It was much better organized and the
crowd much to my surprise was still at about a million. Ethan
and I stood in the same area as we did four years earlier. Time
flew by quickly as we watched Joe Biden and Obama sworn in
for a second term. A second inauguration is never as exciting as
the first, but it still defines an era in American history. The
crowd at the inauguration was excited. It was a cold morning on

the west side of the capitol a couple hours before the
inauguration, but the sun was attempting to rise above the
Cannon Office Building to the east. The crowd continued to flow
in steadily and after a while it was quite tight on the Capitol lawn.
The greatest part of this inauguration was you could just see the
pride in the large African American population that attended.
Going to both Obama inaugurations were some of the greatest
history I have ever witnessed. Too many Americans say I didn't
vote for that president so I would never go to the inauguration. I
don't go to only history I agree with. American history is
fascinating no matter what it is. I am proud to experience all that
I have with disregard to what it is. Obama is my president even
if I didn't vote for him. I feel so fortunate to have witnessed both
inaugurations of our first African American President.

1.   *Presidential Inaugurations, Paul F. Boller, Jr. Harcourt press, 2001.*

CHAPTER THIRTEEN
*SOMETIMES THE SMALLEST PIECES OF
HISTORY ARE THE BEST*

FIRST LADY AND SENATOR

Like her or not, one of the most historic figures of our time is
Hilary Clinton. Legal counsel during the Watergate hearings,
first lady of Arkansas, First Lady of the United States, United
States Senator, Presidential Candidate, and Secretary of State. Of
course, I would not dismiss her chances of being the next
president of the United States.   I have met Clinton three times
during my historic travels. One was at a banquet where she was
given an award and the other while she was Secretary of State
after a speech. However, the first time in 2001 was the best. It
was a great historic experience.

In January 2001 a small piece of history took place for the very
first time. Hardly anyone noticed. However, to me, it was a
great piece of history. For approximately twenty days Hilary
Clinton was both First Lady and a United States Senator. Late in
her husband's terms as President, she decided to live in New
York so she could run for United States Senate. In the great
carpet bagging tradition of Robert Kennedy who did the same
thing, Clinton would cruise to easy victory and come to represent
New York in the United States Senate.

I was determined to see her in person during her role as a Senator
at the same time she was our First Lady. The window was small,
only approximately twenty days. It may never happen again.

To do so I headed to one of the very first things she did as a
United States Senator; participate in a confirmation hearing of a
cabinet appointment of incoming President George W. Bush.
Confirmation hearings are very interesting to a policy wonk and
historian like me. They are the fulfillment of the Senate's
constitutional duty of "advice and consent" on Presidential
appointments and necessary to provide input into the operation of
the executive and judicial branches of government. These
hearings, where the appropriate Senate Committee recommends

the full Senate confirm or reject a presidential nominee, can be very easy and smooth sailing. Others can be very controversial.

To see the First Lady, and fulfill my goal, I attended a confirmation hearing held by of one of her committees, the Senate Environment and Public Works Committee. As a new senator, it was her first meeting of this committee. The confirmation hearing was of New Jersey Governor Christine Todd Whitman for Secretary of the Environmental Protection Agency. Earlier in the day I tried to enter the hearing, but the line was too long. As I finally entered on my second attempt in the afternoon, coming out of the hearing was civil rights activist Al Sharpton. His "entourage" surrounded him. It was inauguration week and George W. Bush would be sworn in as President in a few days. Sharpton was in Washington D.C. to hold a rally protesting giving the State of Florida electoral votes to Bush, and thus the election. Get over it Al is what I wanted to tell him.

The Committee room was packed and most people in the room were there in part to see the First Lady in action as a Senator. There was an air of excitement in large part it was like Clinton was a mega celebrity that everyone came to see. The media was there to cover her first ever confirmation hearing and first meeting of this committee. Other Committee members included Senators George Voinovich of Ohio, Barbara Boxer of California, and Paul Wellstone of Minnesota. Senator Harry Reid of Nevada chaired the Committee. Today Reid serves as the Senate Majority Leader and along with Senator McConnell of Kentucky are the faces of the modern Senate. Pretty scary faces considering these two individuals are putting the country through a nightmare.

The first Lady stood out in the room as she sat in her place as one of the lowest ranking members of the Committee. Like so many in the audience, I focused most of my attention on Mrs. Clinton. Unlike with other Senators, a few Secret Service agents stood nearby. Governor Whitman's hearing had started earlier in the day and I would watch about the last hour and half of it. Senator Voinovich mentioned during his comments how Ohio utilities are in compliance with current standards. Mrs. Clinton made a favorable comment about his statement. Another senator feeding off the joking around said Voinovich and Clinton could co-sponsor a Clinton-Voinovich Bill on some topic environmental topic. The First Lady joked; it would be a Voinovich-Clinton bill. I "understand seniority, she said.

Other business was pretty normal. Senator Boxer requested certain questions be answered by Whitman by the following Monday and others within six months. During the day Whitman promised a strong federal role "in efforts to improve air and water quality and to clean up toxic waste sites." She also expressed the opinion that "more can be accomplished through cooperation than by taking polluters to court or issuing stiff fines." "We will offer the carrot first, but will not retire the stick."

At the close of the hearing was a neat piece of history to witness. The chair welcomed the two new members of the Committee including Clinton. He formally welcomed Mrs. Clinton to her first ever confirmation hearing. The hearing was then adjourned.

The press, with me ahead of them quickly walked toward the First Lady as she stood behind her chair in the front of the room. As I walked toward Clinton, I first grabbing Governor Whitman's name tent from the table where she testified. While I made it up front, Governor Whitman left through a nearby door. Wellstone, Clinton, and Boxer huddled for a minute in private conversation with me in earshot.   The reporters then made their way up front to speak with Mrs. Clinton. She was still standing behind her seat and a small press conference ensued for about five minutes. I was right in the middle of it and just a couple feet away. The questions were mixed but included her dual roles. It was a media circus and the other Senators were basically ignored. Hilary Clinton was the star. The other Committee members left the room inconspicuously.

Following the impromptu press conference, Clinton started to walk toward the door on the other side of the room, answering questions as she went. It was a short distance and I was still in the front row, listening to all the exchanges. Clinton walked right by me, leaned over, and shook my hand. "How are you doing," she asked. "Very well!" "It is an honor to meet you and good luck as Senator." Mrs. Clinton was very friendly and after her departure, I left the room. A few minutes later, Mrs. Clinton was in the hallway with a large number of reporters in tow. The circus continued. I heard one Senate Aide say to another, "it will be like this from now on." I observed the question and answer session, which took place in the hallway and by a small bank of elevators. The press was very fascinated with the Senator who happens to also be First Lady. They also wanted to know her positions on key issues, many of which she may have avoided as First Lady. The roles of First Lady and a Senator were on full display that cold winter afternoon in Washington D.C. Where a First Lady could be considered a little less partisan a Senator certainly is not. Her policy positions were important and the press was pushing for direction as she undertook her new role. It was a great mob scene with questions being shouted out. Mrs. Clinton's hallway news event ended when her elevator came. Mrs. Clinton seemed right at home as a Senator. She always needed a place of her own in politics and appeared to fit right in. She loved it! Mrs. Clinton was very nice, pleasant and cordial to meet. She was very patient with the press.

After Clinton left, but before leaving myself, I stood by the now late Senator Wellstone as he answered press questions. Wellstone, one of the most liberal Senators, would die the next year in a plane crash while campaigning. His wife and a daughter were also killed.

Whitman sailed through the Committee process and was approved by a 99-0 vote by the full Senate. Mrs. Clinton served until 2009 and resigned to become Secretary of State under President Obama.

In 2008, she ran for President and lost in the primary to Barack Obama. There are indications she will run again for president. Can you imagine Watergate attorney, First lady of Arkansas, First Lady of the United States, U.S. Senator, U.S. Secretary of State, and President of the United States? Like her or not, what a historical figure.

CHAPTER FOURTEEN
*OUTSIDE THE WHITE HOUSE AS WAR IS
DECLARED*

In March of 2003, I took a quiet walk in Rock Creek Park in Washington D.C. It was a beautiful spring day with our nation's capital going about its normal business---sort of. While I was eating a sandwich near the park at a sidewalk café, thousands of individuals were protesting on the Mall the impending War with Iraq.

On Monday March 17th, President George W. Bush said, "Today is a moment of truth for the world." The White House announced the President would address the nation that night. It would be a war speech. The place to be that night was outside the White House. The speech was to begin at 8:00 p.m. but I arrived at the White House at 6:45. In front of the White House on Pennsylvania Avenue was a very small crowd. The small size was a surprise. There was one group of organized protestors that formed a circle and it numbered no more than fifteen. They sang several songs whose titles are now lost to history. Walking up and down the street was a lone lady protesting by herself. She pulled behind herself a red wagon full of baby dolls that were made to look injured. It was meant to symbolize the babies she thought would be killed by President Bush if he went forward with the war. Another lady held a sign calling for the impeachment of President Bush. I called home quickly and my family was tuned to the television, as were most Americans, getting ready for the speech. Over the west wing of the White House camera lights dominated the scene. One young man, through the White House fence, started yelling in the direction of the lights. "The news media is only telling Bush's side of the story," echoed through the otherwise quiet streets. A couple guards watched nearby. He yelled this for fifteen minutes. The police let him go on, as they should, but did talk to him once. He was allowed to continue yelling.

I took a walk completely around the White House to see if anything was happening elsewhere and there wasn't.

Pennsylvania Avenue was the center of attention. As the lights
shown through the windows of the upstairs Presidential
residence, President Bush was downstairs preparing for the
speech of his life. Traffic was congested around the White House
because, two days earlier, a North Carolina farmer drove his
tractor into the reflecting pool on the National Mall and he was
still there. The fear was he held explosives, but the event ended a
couple days later without incident.

As the time for the speech grew closer, activity in front of the
White House was no different than it had been before. A few
more people joined the one organized group of protestors. The
police said beginning at 8:00 p.m., the time of the speech,
protestors could no longer just stand still as they had been. They
had to keep moving. The protestors moved in unison across the
street to Lafayette Park and I joined in the march. The group had
one radio in order to listen to the speech. Once on the edge of the
park, the protestors sat down as I stood nearby. The radio was
placed on the ground and turned up as loud as it would go. A
businessman stopped as he was walking by. No one else was
nearby except for the lone anti-nuclear weapon protestor that has
been in Lafayette Park for many years.

The President began and everyone sat in silence. There was little
talking during the entire speech. There was no debate or
discussion. They wanted to hear what the President said.
President Bush said he would attack Iraq with the "full force and
might" of the United States if Saddam Hussein does not flee Iraq
within 48 hours. The President had set the country on a sure path
to war, if the ultimatum was not accepted. The protestors lit
candles. One girl asked me if I wanted one. I took one but after a
minute, it blew out. The President said, "The tyrant will soon be
gone; the day of your liberation is near. It is too late for Saddam
Hussein to remain in power. It is not too late for the Iraqi military
to act with honor and protect your country; by permitting the
peaceful entry of coalition forces to eliminate weapons of mass
destruction." As a result of this ultimatum, a "heightened watch"
for terrorism was declared and the terrorism alert was raised to
"code orange," the second highest level. During the speech, I
constantly watched the White House. The lights of course, were

still on and the building looked as beautiful as ever. I often looked at the front door; one I have gone through several times. Behind it was Entrance Hall and then Cross Hall. It was from Cross Hall that the President spoke. A handful of people walked in front of the White House as the President spoke.

Still, I was very struck by how few people were there. The President of the United States was declaring war as the nation's capital seemed completely normal. In some of the tall buildings, on the other side of the Park, the top floors seemed crowded with people.

Inside the White House, the President said, "All the decades of deceit and cruelty have now reached an end. Saddam Hussein and his sons must leave Iraq within 48 hours. Their refusal to do so will result in military conflict commencing at a time of your choosing. For their own safety, all foreign nationals, including journalists and inspectors should leave Iraq immediately." It was as Bush spoke these words that I felt the greatest sense of history.

Forty eight hours later we were at war.

Following the speech, people quietly went on their way. I left, walking down to the Capitol City Brewery for dinner. It was crowded but I didn't have to wait for a table. The talk of the restaurant was the speech, but no one would know by looking that the nation was on the brink of war.

The next morning was a breakfast event featuring Senator Jim Bunning and a lunch event featuring Kentucky Congressmen Ken Lucas and Hal Rogers. Prior to the lunch I had a meeting with Congressman Lucas. The Congressman was in his last term, choosing not to run for re-election in 2004. He had promised to only serve three terms. Lucas previously served on the Board of Directors of the Northern Kentucky Area Development District, my employer. Lucas talked about how busy the Congress was with the impending war and that the war is the main order of business. He had just attended a briefing on the war. The Congressman laughed when I told him about my experiences from the night before and sarcastically said the protest and a picture of me in it would be a good photo on the front of *The Kentucky Post*. As my reason for being in DC was a lobbying trip, we discussed some business including the replacement of the Brent Spence Bridge and a road project in Carroll County.

Clearly this speech doesn't compare to any Roosevelt gave during World War II or any by war presidents including Wilson, LBJ, or Lincoln. However, to discount this war, no matter what your opinion, would be a disservice to the men and women who fought it. Thousands would lose their lives. Hussein would be out of power immediately and his sons would be dead quickly. America rejoiced. I supported the war, but did so under false pretense. The President either lied or was just simply wrong. I prefer to believe he was wrong. He said Hussein had weapons of mass destruction and that is why we went in. He was wrong. He said it was because of Hussein's involvement in 9/11. He was wrong. So why did we go to war. We didn't find any weapons of mass destruction and if we did they probably would have had "Made in the USA" stamped on them. Bush declared "Mission Accomplished" within a few months. In other words, we won. Funny thing, the war went on for almost another decade. At the same time we went into two wars, Bush lowered taxes-- the first time in history this happened during a war. Our deficit skyrocketed (not as much as since he left office) but a record for the time. We were duped. However, with all that said, it was pretty satisfying to see Hussein swing from a rope.

So what was launched from the White House on that March evening? Was it the beginning of a transformation of the Middle East that will take decades to see the true results? Was democracy's flame lit? Or was it another example of American imperialism run amok? Was it another reason for people to hate us? I still can't tell you why we went in because the President's story changed so much. Wasn't Afghanistan the real problem? Either way President Bush put us at war that night in DC. With little worldwide support, and conflicting and inaccurate reasons, the capital city went about its business as usual. It was like nothing significant was happening. Did anyone really care?

CHAPTER FIFTEEN

THE DEDICATION OF THE WORLD WAR II MEMORIAL
A SIMPLE FATHER AND SONS' STORY

The story that follows is basically as written almost ten years ago, except for some details nobody outside my family would care about. I want to encourage parents to occasionally take their children on out-of-the ordinary trips. Some trips are once in a lifetime unique events a parent and child can experience. They can develop memories that will last a lifetime, and I encourage all parents to write stories with details to be passed down for generations. This is one such story.

On Thursday May 27, 2004, I left home with my sons, Andrew and Ethan, for a drive to Washington DC for the dedication of the World War II Memorial. World War II has always fascinated me, and as a child I would let my homework pile up but would have no trouble reading a book about the great conflict. In Ludlow, one of my favorite childhood imaginary games was to play war, me and a couple friends against a few thousand Germans. Our guns were sticks and we played at Pigeon Point, a beautiful hill in Ludlow with tremendous vistas of Cincinnati. Today the hill is covered with condos. The Children's Home in Devou Park was the German headquarters. We always won the battle, despite being out numbered by a few thousand. My favorite movie growing up was *Patton* and once I visited his grave in Luxembourg. My wife still laughs at the 20 pictures I took of his grave from every angle. His grave is marked by a simple cross and one picture would have worked. Growing up, my favorite movies were World War II Classics and I loved watching them with my friend, Kevin Kelly.

My dad generally talked about his World War II service, but I never really asked much about it. Perhaps because he usually talked about the time he was in Cleveland at Crile Military Hospital, and it wasn't as exciting as being in the European campaign. However, his service was very important and I remain very proud of what he did in serving his Country. In going to the dedication of the World War II Memorial, Dad was on my mind,

On the day of the ceremony, I wore a t-shirt with his picture on it. He was in uniform and looked handsome. I would be born around fifteen years after the picture was taken.

The first full day in the nation's capital, we arrived at the Mall and walked toward the Washington Monument passing under a large sign that read National World War II Reunion. On the way to visit the new World War II Memorial for the first time, we came across an elderly man walking slowly. He said he was a veteran and had fought in Normandy. Although we would talk to many veterans on this trip, for some now unknown reason we didn't really talk with this guy. A few minutes later we entered , for the first time, the long overdue memorial to the men and women who fought in World War II.

Bob and his two sons, Andrew (left) and Ethan (right),
at the dedication of the World War II Memorial

President Clinton signed the World War II Memorial authorization legislation into law in 1993. Six years before, an Ohio Veteran asked his Congresswoman why there was no memorial to the veterans of World War II. Sixteen million Americans participated in the various services during World War II and approximately 400,000 died. Like the Vietnam Memorial, it is important that the veterans be recognized that their service was not in vain. "The site chosen proved to be controversial as many believed it would interrupt the unbroken view between the Washington Monument and the Lincoln Memorial." [1] The big question was, can a memorial be constructed to effectively memorialize an entire generation of individuals who fought the greatest conflict in the history of mankind? I was interested to see for myself.

We entered the Memorial on 17th Street. The stage for the next day's dedication was on the opposite side of the street and chairs filled the shadow of the Washington Monument. It was early in the morning and there were a lot of people, but not so crowded as to cause any problems. It had rained the afternoon and evening before, but now the early morning sun shined. There was plenty of room to walk around and enjoy the grandeur of the monument. Immediately upon entering I was struck by several things. One was the beauty of the monument. It shined with its new granite. The other was its grandeur. The large pillars and the North and South entrances represented a strength to me that described the World War II generation. The men and women who fought in World War II were very strong. They sacrificed so much of their personal lives to fight a war in a foreign land, were brave and did their duty when called upon. Their strength was evident in the memorial. The reflecting pool and the entire Memorial's position between the Lincoln Memorial and the Washington Monument spoke volumes on the importance of World War II. The controversy carried no real weight with me. However, the greatest part of the memorial was not the granite or the grandeur. It was the veterans. Walking around were veterans from the war, many of them in their sixty-year-old uniforms. It was a site to behold and I was amazed at the walking history that surrounded me. The time was around 9:40 a.m.

Immediately upon entering there was a group of veterans at the main entrance. They were posing for a picture and we talked for several minutes with an Air Force Vietnam veteran from Minnesota that won the Bronze Star. He talked with Andrew about the Air Force Academy, including grades and extracurricular activities. The veteran told Andrew it was important to play a sport in high school. "The Academy loves sports as criteria", he said. This veteran had his two sons with him. There were many Vietnam Veterans at the memorial this weekend to pay tribute to the World War II generation.

Fifty-six states and territories that united in the war are remembered on pillars around the memorial. When we arrived at Kentucky, there was a man from Pike County. We talked for several minutes and took our picture with him at the pillar. He wore a hat that said "World War II veteran and proud of it." The hat told accurately how he felt. One thing most veterans expressed this weekend was how proud they were of their service, even though it is often said many World War II veterans don't like to talk about what they saw and experienced. During this weekend, all veterans we encounter were more than willing to talk.

We continued our tour by stopping at the Freedom Wall and its 4000 gold stars in honor of the 400,000 Americans who lost their lives in the war. Seeing it for the first time, and with my two boys, was special because we were connected to this spot. We were not only from Kentucky but my father and their grandfather served in this war and my uncle, Bill Schrage, was killed. I couldn't help but feel the connection.

Behind the Pacific section of the memorial was the National World War II Registry. We went over and used one of the computers at a window. We pulled up Schrage and to my surprise my name came up. This Robert J. Schrage was in the U.S. Army Air Corps and from Brooklyn, NY. His daughter Sharon Schrage was listed, which means she entered him into the registry. His activity during the war said, "Flew B-29s during the war. His job was to regulate the flow of gasoline on the plane for the entire mission. His unit received President Truman's Presidential citation for the longest bombardment mission, 22 hours. He also received an air medal with cluster." My Dad, Richard J. Schrage was also listed. I had entered him about a month or so before, including his picture.   My Father was born in 1917 in Covington, KY and served on the home front the entire war.   His last assignment was as an x-ray technician at Crile Military Hospital in Cleveland, Ohio where he met my mother.

We continued to walk around the memorial after visiting the registry. Upon reentering the memorial, we immediately looked out from the Pacific overview, just like we did the Atlantic on the other side. As we did an elderly gentleman was standing alone looking out. He stood there for some time, reflecting. He had on a yellow vest filled with patches and it indicated he was a submarine veteran and served on the USS Neches (AO-5 and the USS Sperry). He was from Texas and a member of a submarine association chapter from that state. This was one of my favorite memories of the trip. The USS Neches was built in 1919 at the Boston Navy Yard and was commissioned in 1920. The oilier was headed to Pearl Harbor when the base was attacked by Japan. It then ran supplies back and forth from San Diego during the crisis. In January 1942, the Neches left Pearl Harbor and was sunk by a Japanese submarine. Fifty-seven people were killed. The veteran we were standing with was a real hero. Like most of the survivors of the Neches, he was assigned to the USS Sperry, which was still under construction. The Sperry served in the Pacific during World War II and in Korea.

We continued walking and stopped at the Guam pillar because it had special meaning to us on this trip. On the way to D.C., we played trivia in the car. None of us knew the capital of Guam and so we kept talking about it. It became a running joke. Ethan was the one who first raised the question even though he didn't know the answer. Thus, we took his picture at the Guam pillar.

At the foot of the walkway coming down from the Pacific side, a park service employee was obtaining signatures of veterans and listing their units for historic purposes. He said it would be placed in the National Archives and so we flipped through the book. Originally a blank book, it was now partially filled with World War II veteran signatures. The park service official was impressed and happy that I was making sure my kids learned about this war and the sacrifices and accomplishments of the World War II generation. Many of the veterans we talked to this weekend said the same thing to us.

At the entrance to the Memorial we had an inspirational discussion with two veterans. They were Korean War Veterans and one was named Andrew Anderson, 67. Andrew was a very nice person, and I believe the first African American Veteran we talked with. Anderson was proud of his service despite the racism that existed in the country and in the armed services. It is amazing to me how African American soldiers served their country despite being treated as second-class citizens. The African American veterans we saw that weekend all were proud of their service. Often overlooked, I think their service helped to slowly turn the tide against racism and their victory in Europe helped set the stage for victory in the fight against inequality at home. Anderson, while a Korean War Veteran, helped tell that story for the first time to my kids, We all took a picture with Anderson in front of the Memorial where it was etched the following: "They fought together as brothers-in-arms. They died together and now they sleep side by side. To them we have a solemn obligation." This quote from Admiral Chester Nimetz seemed like the perfect place to have a picture taken with Anderson.

On the way to show my kids the White House, we met a World War II veteran and his daughter. He was very elderly and confined to a wheel chair. His daughter was very proud of his service and excited that we were so interested in meeting him. He survived the Bataan Death March and described it as the living hell it must have been. He says he was lucky to survive it, but in hindsight was a better person because of it. Like all the veterans we met, we shook hands. Following the Battle of Bataan, the Japanese forced American and Filipino prisoners of war to march 80 miles to a POW Camp. The POWs were treated brutally and in many cases murdered along the march. Very little water or food was supplied and of course, many died. Following the war, the Death March was found to be a war crime by an allied commission. The gentleman we met on the street corner was lucky to be alive and survived one of the most brutal events of the war. He was so proud and happy to talk that it made me feel so honored to even be there with him. The fact his daughter was there also, so very proud, made the occasion even more memorable.

We then walked up 17th Street and encountered a large group of protestors outside the Organization of American States. They were chanting and pounding on drums and cans and they were protesting for fair trade. It was 11:35 a.m. and we walked right through the protestors. The kids thought it was different than anything they had seen before. We made it to the White House on the South Side and Ethan liked it a lot. It was really special for him to see this building in person. We had our picture taken sitting on the curb and against the White House fence. Hungry, we walked up town to find a place to eat.

After eating, we took a taxi to the Air and Space Museum, which Andrew was really looking forward to seeing. He had talked about it a lot before coming on the trip. It was a little past 1:00 p.m. and we saw Apollo 11, the Wright Brothers Plane, various World War II planes and weapons, including a Spitfire and a piece of Jimmy Doolittle's plane; and various rockets. Both kids had dog tags made. The highlight for kids, however, was a simulator called "At the Controls." It was a flight simulator doing turns, flipping over, etc. When they were done the first time, they begged to do it again. Andrew, who was dragging a little, came to life. I let them go again and they were very excited.

At 3:00 p.m. we were in the history tent on the Mall, back at the World War II Homecoming event. On the Mall were various tents, each with a different theme. They included the Veterans History Project, Building the Memorial, Preserving Memories, Reunion Hall, Wartime Stories, Family Activities, Capitol Canteen, and Veterans Services. Surrounding the tents was a Homecoming stage for entertainment and display of military vehicles from World War II. We visited everything!

The History Project was perhaps my favorite. In it was a stage where veterans made presentations. However, that was not the best part. In the tent, veterans were mingling and it was easy to talk to each, all with great stories. In one section of the tent, volunteers sat at computers and interviewed veterans and documented stories. I was honored to stand there and watch all those veterans telling their stories. This alone was worth the trip to Washington and my sons also appreciated the significance of the site. We talked with many veterans. One was Thomas Lowery. Lowery, " a native of San Antonio, Texas enlisted in the U.S. Army Corps in 1942 and was assigned to Kelly Field and happily joined the drum and bugle corps. A month later, he was transferred to the airplane mechanic school at Lincoln, NB, and then onto Army specialized training program in engineering at Howard University, Washington, D.C. Lowery served next in Florida and was then was sent to Michigan and assigned to the 477th Medium Bombardment Group. The group was based at Goodman Field, KY with various short-term training assignments at other Army facilities around the country and accrued the best safety record in the 1st Air Force. Following the war Lowery returned to Washington, D.C., became an electrician and continued to work in the field. (Veterans History Project Stories)."

Lowery was a Tuskegee Airman and served from 1939-1945. He was the first Tuskegee Airman we met.

The second was Col. Charles McGee. USAF (Ret). "A native of Cleveland, OH, McGee was a student at the University of Illinois when WWII interrupted his education. He was sworn into enlisted reserve in October 1942 and entered U.S. Army Air Corps flight training a month later. He was commissioned a second Lieutenant in June, 1943 graduating in Class 43-F, Tuskegee Army Air Field, McGee became a command pilot with over 6,100 total hours and flew fighter aircraft in Italy during the WWII; in the Philippines and Korea and in Vietnam. In Vietnam he flew 172 combat missions and according to Wikipedia, flew 409 fighter combat missions, the highest of any three-war Air Force aviator in history. Following his 30 years of military service, he held leadership positions in the Interstate Securities Company Financial Corporation and later served as manager of Kansas City, MO. Downtown Airport. He retired from private industry in 1982 to pursue community interests and has been active in numerous local and national organizations." McGee was very gracious and spoke a long time with Andrew about the academies and a military career. He talked about the importance of excellent grades, and other activities to do now in order to be prepared for a military career. In his career McGee was awarded the Distinguished Flying Cross, the Bronze medal and a Legion of Merit, among others.

Lt. Col Lee Archer, Jr., USAF (Ret) was "chairman and CEO of Archer Associates, and President, Organization Publishing Company, joined the U.S. Air Force and entered flight training at Tuskegee Army Air Field, graduating as a Fighter Pilot 1, Class 43-G. He joined the 302 Fighter Squadron of the 322n Fighter Group and went on to become a fighter "ACE." In 1944, he became one of four "triplers" who destroyed three Me-109s on one mission. After 29 years of military service, Archer joined General Foods Corp. in 1970, was named vice president of General Foods for North Street Capitol Corporation in 1975, and in 1980 was elected GF Corporation Vice President. He is a member of the Veterans History Project Five Star Council."

We had wanted to meet some Tuskegee Airman on this trip and had now met three: Lowery, McGee and Archer. Tuskegee Air Base in Alabama was the training base for the Air Force of Negro troops. This segregated base was another example of the Air Force racial discrimination of black soldiers. Commander of the Air Force, General H.H. "Hap" Arnolds' racist policies excluded black pilots because they would be ranked higher than some whites. Tuskegee was created to have an all-black squadron. Using black airmen was forced upon Arnold. The base was built in order to keep Negro trainees from being integrated into a white base just 40 miles away (Maxwell Field). The Tuskegee Airman are great heroes and not only did they fight for their country, they did so in the face of racism that came not only from some of the people they were fighting to protect, but also from the military itself. It is an amazing story that these individuals served their country so well under these circumstances. They fought two wars at the same time: one oversees and one in America. I am proud to have met them and for Andrew and Ethan to know their story. I-75, running through my home of Northern Kentucky is dedicated to these brave airmen.

On a corner by the Smithsonian, a street vendor was selling film and other souvenirs. At this spot was a Code Talker. Both kids have been watching a movie called *Windtalkers* that recently came out about the Code Talkers and what they did during the war. This gentleman was with his wife and granddaughter. His name was Merrill L. Sandoval, Cpl U.S. MC 5th and 2nd Marine

Division (1943-1946). Mr. Sandoval lived in Tuba, AZ. Merrill is Naaneesh'tezhi' Dine'e' (Zuni Clan) born for Tl'aaschi'l (Red Bottom People Clan). He served in the Hawaiian Islands, Saipan, Iwo Jima, and in the Japanese Occupation. He served from 1943-1946. These were some of the hardest fought campaigns of the wars, particularly Iwo Jima and Saipan. The movie *Windtalkers* is about the battle at Saipan. The Navajo language was used to communicate and send top-secret messages because the enemy could not break it. It was very successful and the Code Talkers served an important role, as Mr. Sandoval says, to "defeat the enemy." He took part in every marine landing in the Pacific Ocean theater of World War II from 1943-1945. Like so many people of this generation, Sandoval told us he enlisted at the age of seventeen. He died in 2008 at the age of 82 and received full military honors and the Navajo nation flew flags at half-mast in his honor.[2]

Bob with a Navajo 'code talker' during the World War II Memorial dedication

Back on the Mall, my son, Andrew, particularly liked all the military vehicles and took pictures of each one. Andrew and Ethan posed in a jeep and we spent considerable time looking at the array of World War II military vehicles that were on display.

In Reunion Hall were large bulletin boards divided by branches of service and broken down into units. World War II veterans were sitting at tables in the middle of the room sharing stories and meeting up with old buddies from the war. Some were just talking with people with similar experiences or served in the same place. It was an incredible site and on the boards a veteran could leave a message for somebody they were looking to find. We spent some time reading the messages and I put one up looking for information from anybody that served at Crile Military Hospital in Cleveland the same time as my father. I never received a reply.

At the end of our first day, we headed to the subway, getting on at the Smithsonian Station for our ride to the park and ride lot. For supper we bought pizza and took it to the motel room.

We awoke early the next day, Saturday May 29, 2004, the day of the dedication of the World War II Memorial. We bought some donuts and drinks and drove the car to Washington and easily found a parking spot at the Crystal City Mall and took the subway the short distance into town. We arrived early, some four or five hours before the 2:00 p.m. ceremony. For a couple hours we revisited the tents from the day before and did some new activities. We each received "marching orders" in the form of a small booklet and set out to complete the tasks. In it we had to "break a code," learn about rationing on the homefront, identify enemy fighter planes, and other tasks. When we completed our orders we had to go to a station and have it reviewed for accuracy. When approved, we went to another station and received a medal for our efforts. We each wore our medals the rest of the day.

Walking around the Mall this day, we encountered many veterans of World War II and had many exciting discussions. Our favorite by far was a guy named Jason Lee. He was dressed in his World War II uniform and was a short guy. He was funny and very personable and a former Marine. He had been stationed in Guam. Another Guam related story that made Ethan happy. Lee could remember that every night planes took off every 22 seconds, all night long. One night this did not happen. It was all-quiet and the silence was noted this particular evening. Later he found out that the Enola Gay took off to drop the first atomic bomb on Japan. The date was August 6, 1945. The Enola Gay took off from Tinian Island in the Mariana Islands. Ethan and Mr. Lee got along great and he was about Ethan's height with his hat on. Mr. Lee was always smiling and said to Ethan "Semper Fi", the marine slogan meaning "Always Loyal". We sat on a bench with Mr. Lee and he made us laugh because he had a pleasant and humorous personality. He told us stories including answering Ethan's question of, "What is the capital of Guam?" "Hagatna," he responded, ending the long unanswered question. Our time with Lee was perhaps our greatest experience with a World War II veteran on the trip and when I think of the dedication, I often think of Jason Lee.

After a time of walking around doing things, we headed into the roped off area where we would watch the dedication ceremony. It would be nice to say we saw the ceremony with our own eyes, but that is not true. Our section allowed us seats, but we would be watching the ceremony on a large screen. We did have live entertainment on the stage by the screen and our section had many World War II veterans in it. It was a hot and sunny day. Near our seats was another Code Talker from Arizona. He was in his Navajo dress just like Sandoval the day before. Next to me sat a World War II bombardier. By about noon, the large area we were in was mostly filled and World War II era music played over loud speakers. There were lots of hats on veterans that indicated their duty during the war. Many veterans wore their uniform. "God Bless America" was sung, as was, "America" and "This Land is Your Land." Upon entering the seated section, a package was given to each person and it included several items including a flag, program, and commemorative medal.

We watched the ceremony on the large screen, burnt from the hot sun beating down on our heads. After 59 years a memorial to the World War II generation was finally completed. Construction started just seven days before the attacks on New York City on September 11, 2001. It took less than three years to complete. Speakers included Tom Brokow, author of *The Greatest Generation*; Actor Tom Hanks, National Spokesman for the World War II Memorial Campaign; Senator Bob Dole, National Chair for the Memorial Campaign; and President George W. Bush.

What really was honored that day was the spirit of the World War II veterans. Today our world is still free because of this generation. As expressed by the great historian Steven Ambrose:

"A bright image of the legacy of World War II came to me from a veteran. He told me that he felt he had done his part in helping change the twentieth century from darkness to light. In 1945, it was difficult to believe in human progress. The two world wars had made a mockery of the Enlightenment idea of progress. In 1945, one had to believe that the outcome of the scientific and technological revolution that had inspired the idea of progress would be destroyed in a nuclear holocaust. But slowly, surely the spirit of those GIs handing out candy and helping bring democracy to their foreign enemies spread, and by the beginning of this century it is democracy, not dictatorship, that is on the march."[3]

Ambrose and I both feel nobody has done more to help spread freedom and democracy around the world than this generation. My sons and I were there to see this generation honored. It was an educational trip for us all. A trip where we participated in a solemn and historic remembrance; a father and sons' trip none of us will ever forget.

It was a special time all around.

1.   *World War Two Memorial, 2010, Maureen Picard Robins, Rourke Publishing,*

2.   *Wikipedia, Merill Sandoval*

3.   *To America, Simon and Schuster 2002*

CHAPTER SIXTEEN
ROSA PARKS DIES

There are not many people as good as Rosa Parks. She was born in Tuskegee, Alabama on February 4, 1913 and is one of the most important figures of my lifetime. She has been called the "Mother of the Modern Civil Rights Movement." On December 1, 1955, four years before my birth, Rosa Parks refused to give up her seat on a Montgomery, Alabama bus to a white passenger. This violated Montgomery's racial segregation laws. This single act of courage led to a dramatic change in America. Dr. Martin Luther King, Jr. organized a boycott of the city's bus company. Seventy percent of the ridership was African American. Less than a year later, the Supreme Court ruled the segregation of the bus company unconstitutional. The day after the court order was issued, the strike was settled.[1] Not only did it spark the modern civil rights movement, it also has served as a reminder and refresher on American freedoms that had never been available to all citizens. Parks is a true and humble American hero that has done much for our country. Not only did she change law but eventually changed attitudes. The part of her story inspiring me the most is how this simple act of courage had such an impact. Other great leaders such as in the women's movement like Elizabeth Cady Stanton and Susan B. Anthony made their impact through speech after speech, rally after rally. It was not until years after their deaths that women received the right to vote.

Parks' very simple but brave act inspired the Montgomery Bus Boycott. As Daniel Wheeler of the Citizens Flag Alliance, Inc. said, "It could have been a December evening like countless others. Yet, once too often Rosa Parks was told to stand in the back of the bus. All of the indignities she had suffered personally and vicariously seemed to well up from the very pit of her stomach. All of the evil that had been thrust upon her people; all of those times she had bit her tongue when justice demanded that she speak -- all of that and more was quietly reflected in one simple phrase: "No. I'm not moving." [2]

History was changed forever.

Rosa Parks died on October 24, 2005 in Detroit, Michigan. Her death sparked a week of mourning that included her becoming the first woman and civilian to lie in honor in the United States Capitol Rotunda. In the days before, there was a public viewing in Montgomery, Alabama. After lying in state in Washington D.C., her body was immediately flown to Detroit to lie in the rotunda at the Charles H. Wright Museum of African History on Warren Avenue.

I decided to drive to Detroit to witness this piece of history and I left on Tuesday morning November 1, 2005 driving straight up I-75 and arriving in Detroit in the late morning. The Warren Avenue sidewalks were busy with people walking to and from the museum where Rosa Parks was lying. It was cold and I wore a heavy jacket. On the Plaza in front of the Museum, people were milling around. The crowd was not large and the first thing I noticed on the plaza was the Cleveland Avenue bus. This was the bus Rosa Parks was on when she refused to give up her seat. It is owned by the Henry Ford Museum and moved there for the day as a way to honor the memory and life of Rosa Parks. On the front and one side of the bus was a dark memorial cloth or drape. Also on the plaza was the Swanson Funeral Home hearse that brought Rosa Parks to this place and would take her to the memorial service the next day. The hearse was a very unique antique vehicle. I touched the hearse several times in various places thus feeling connected in some small way to the proceedings.

After ten minutes on the plaza, I walked to the back of the museum to get in line to go into the rotunda. The line was long but could have been much worse. It took me about an hour and a half to get in. The line was made up of mostly African Americans. Clearly, Rosa Parks is an icon to the African American community but she should also be seen as a hero to whites for showing us how America had never completely lived up to its tremendous ideas. She made us all better. I was disappointed more whites were not there. I listened carefully to the conversations while waiting in line. The crowd was very respectful of the situation and was made up of people of all ages. People told stories of Parks and discussed the current state of race relations. They were all negative comments. As a white middle class and middle-aged man, relations didn't seem so bad and our perspectives were entirely different. Now, from my perspective, we have made tremendous progress in the last sixty years with still much to do. However, as I optimistically looked at the progress; the people waiting in line negatively saw unfinished business. As I looked at an infrastructure of anti-discrimination laws; the people in line saw the need for more affirmative action. As I saw some of the civil rights leaders of the day as bigots themselves or as race baiters; the people in line saw heroes. As I have run organizations free of discrimination; those in line saw me as a white man incapable of understanding. As I see it one of the biggest stumbling blocks to good race relations is the constant calling of people as racists depending on their politics. The people in line see liberals as doing no wrong and conservatives as doing no right. Thinking today of the line I stood in eight years earlier; it is clear to me the African American leaders of today are just as much of a stumbling block as anyone in the march to equality. Today, African American leaders such as Jessie Jackson or Al Sharpton act as thought police. You can only be liberal and African American. A conservative African American is an Uncle Tom, or a traitor to the cause. Think of Herman Cain, Colin Powell, Clarence Thomas, or Walter Williams. They have all been called these names. Why? Because they have different thoughts. One test of whether true equality exists is when the African American leaders allow free thought among their constituents without being called names. Another will be to stop calling people racist who are not. Four people I know, none of who are racist in anyway, were called so by white liberals when they indicated they were voting for Romney over Obama in the 2012 Presidential election. Oh, by the way, I was one. We need to call out racism when it shows its ugly head; however, the throwing out of the term irresponsibly only makes whites jaded to the term and the cause. It is a hindrance to real efforts to eradicate the evil of racism.

Outside the museum there were laughs and friends saying hello to each other. The line started the evening before about 9:00 p.m. and it had been steady ever since. Near me in line was an artist from Detroit named Willie Harris who quietly held his painting of Rosa. He held it in respect to Parks and never said a word. Immediately behind me was Vernon Griffin who was blind. He had a black Labrador dog named Nero. He was with Alice Landino, 30, a mobility instructor at Detroit Receiving Hospital. She had brought him down for the visitation. He wouldn't have missed it for anything.

Upon entering the museum, I was immediately handed an obituary card with a beautiful picture of Rosa Parks on one side. It was nice to be in from the cold but the warmth of Parks' soul was what dominated the surroundings. A couple volunteers held tissue boxes at the entrance and a few people cried. The rotunda was gorgeous, highlighted by a spectacular 100 foot by 55 foot glass dome. The small mahogany coffin stood in the mammoth rotunda but still dominated the room. All eyes were focused on Rosa Parks and an honor guard stood by. I walked past slowly, pausing for a brief second. Mostly I remember her small physical stature, small knit cap with a stripe, and blanket draped over her body. Her face was small. While noticing the surroundings, I still looked at Rosa Parks' body the entire time. After passing the coffin, compelled, I turned to look again. Even though this piece of history was a solemn occasion, I could not help but be excited about seeing her. My thoughts were not on the sadness of her death but on the greatness of her life. Present that day was not a body, but a soul who made a difference; not a still body in death, but an icon of American history.

Back outside the warmth of the rotunda gave into the cold November air but I never noticed the difference. I was inspired by the story of this great American and oblivious to the cold because of both my excitement and reverence of the occasion. I had paid my respects to Rosa Parks, a person that through one simple act, changed America forever.

1.   *The 100 Most Influential Americans, Running Press, 2008.*

2.   *Just Plain Tired of Being Pushed Around, By Daniel S. Wheeler, President, The Citizens Flag Alliance, Inc.*

CHAPTER SEVENTEEN
THE LIZ CARROLL TRIAL

As I sat in the woods during a winter morning in 2007, I was struck as always by the beauty of the majestic Ohio River flowing through the valley below. Several hours later, I sat at a picnic table on the opposite shore in Rising Sun, Indiana, looking across at my home town of Rabbit Hash, KY. The story I write about is contrary to the beauty that surrounded me. It is a story of a day in the trial of Liz Carroll, an accused murderer in one of the most sensational cases in Greater Cincinnati history. Local history events are not something I generally write about. I go to events on a national scale; however, this one compelled me.

MURDER

In August of 2006 Marcus Fiesel, a child with autism, was bound from his neck to above his feet and left in a small baby bed in a closet. His foster parents, Liz and David Carroll, along with a friend, Amy Baker, left for a weekend family reunion in Williamstown, Kentucky. When they returned some 36 hours later, Marcus was dead. The Carroll's reported him missing after the body was disposed. They said Marcus went missing from an Anderson Township Park after Liz passed out because of not taking her medicine A community man-hunt for the child began and publicity was tremendous. Liz Carroll held an emotional news conference pleading for the boy's return. The body had been burned by David Carroll at a spot identified by Baker, an old chimney near where she grew up. Amy and David then disposed of the remains by throwing them off a bridge in Maysville, KY.

THE TRIAL

On Monday February 19, 2007, Presidents Day, I attended the trial of Liz Carroll, as the key prosecution witness, Amy Baker, was set to testify. It would be the most dramatic day of the trial. Anticipation was high for the entire community. Arriving at the

Clermont County Courthouse around 8:00 a.m., I was one hour early for the scheduled start of the important day. One media truck was outside. Upon entering the courthouse, I went through the security screen very fast and was the only visitor in sight. Opening the courtroom door, I found myself in a small room and on the right was the witness waiting room. Entering a second door I found myself at the back of the small gallery in a beautiful and stately courtroom. Parts of its appearance was recognizable because of the extensive news coverage and by watching some of the trial live on the Internet

After sitting, a bailiff asked me to move because it was reserved for security. The security was assigned, for this day, because the Sims family (Liz Carroll's family) would occupy this row of seats. I sat on the end of the bench next to the aisle. The media reported later in the evening that the courtroom was filled an hour before the trial resumed. This was not correct, although it filled pretty quickly. Sitting to my right was Norm Aubin, Amy Baker's court appointed attorney and he had been in the courtroom when I arrived. Directly in front of me sat Audrey Sims, the mother of the defendant, Liz Carroll; Toni Hines, a former relation by marriage; and Cathy Adams, the attorney for David Carroll. David Carroll's murder trial was scheduled to begin in a few weeks. Also in the row in front of me, and to the left, was Debbie Hounshell, David Carroll's mother, and Cherice Adkins, his step-sister. Other notables in the courtroom included Bill Cunningham, WLW Radio personality, Phil Heimlich, former Hamilton County Commissioner, and Mike Allen, former Hamilton County prosecutor. Before the trial began, Heimlich got out of his seat, approximately seven or eight times---never once saying excuse me or thanks for getting everyone in the row up again. Heimlich, the son of the inventor of the Heimlich maneuver, and Allen were covering the trial for the media. Also in the room, just across the aisle from me, was the mother of Carrie Culbertson, a murder victim whose body has never been found. The Culbertson missing person and subsequent murder trial was a famous case in the area and it was also based in Clermont County.

As I waited for an hour for the trial to begin, the family waited patiently. Cathy Baker was talkative most of the time. Her husband came into the courtroom with her, but had to sit in the back of the room, on the opposite side. She sat directly in front of me. Adams talked to Heimlich and said she would be seeking to have David Carroll's trial moved to a different venue because of all the publicity from Liz's trial. Heimlich reminded her about how rare and difficult that would be. Adams had one hand wrapped because, according to her, the result of a car accident. She said, her thumb had nerve damage and would need surgery.

CARROLL ENTERS THE COURTROOM

Around 9:00 a.m. my anticipation to see Liz Carroll was finally relieved when the accused murderer walked into the courtroom. Wearing her hair straight with small round glasses gave the impression of a woman far more educated than was the case. She was wearing a dark pants suit with white shirt. She made no eye contact with anyone, taking her seat about ten feet in front of me.

A little after 9:00 a.m., the Judge entered the courtroom and the defense had questions for two jurors. Judge Robert Ringland then brought them in one at a time. The defense attorney, Greg Cohen, wanted to know why they pointed in the direction of the defense table yesterday. It was believed they wanted the podium moved so they could watch Liz Carroll's reactions. This is exactly what the first juror said, which was confirmed by the second juror moments later.

The entire jury was then brought in. Lee Carty, a seventy-two year old retired paper manufacturer, was the first to enter, taking his regular seat in the first row, first seat, closest to the audience.

AMY BAKER TESTIFIES

Judge Ringland was now ready to begin and Clermont County Assistant Prosecutor, Daniel "Woody" Beyer, called his first witness, Amy Baker. As I sat on the aisle seat, Baker walked into the courtroom, sometimes looking down, passing within a foot of me. This image of her entering the courtroom became the most played and important video and image of the entire trial. As it was played over and over again, even months later, I was right in the middle of the image, following her entrance with my eyes. Baker appeared much different than her mug shot. She appeared nervous (which is not a surprise) and certainly was not as pretty as the mug shot. This is odd, but her mug shot is an attractive picture. She was a little heavy set and wore a yellow jacket and scarf. Her turtle neck provided a good indication of the cold weather outside and as she raised her hand to be sworn in, her jacket cuff extended up above her wrist.

An important aspect of the case is that Amy Baker was given full immunity provided she didn't lie on the stand and no new evidence came out that she was involved in the murder. Beyer began by going over the immunity deal, so it would be out on the table. It was obvious Cohen would talk about the deal later. Her testimony lasted a couple hours and it was riveting and disturbing. I, as well as everyone in the courtroom, hung on every word. Sitting directly behind the Carroll family, it was easy to watch their reactions to the testimony. Often, it was a simple shaking of their heads as specific things were said. Once, Cherice Adkins put her face in her hands. Woody Beyer went through a lot of questions about the months and days leading up to the murder. He had a legal pad with the questions written out, and as he asked a question, he would scratch it out. Baker met the Carroll's around March 2005 when she was referred to Liz Carroll's day care business. Soon afterwards, David Carroll made sexual advances on Baker and she eventually moved in with the Carroll's.

According to Baker, Liz Carroll did not want to take Marcus to a family reunion in Kentucky the weekend of August 4, 2005. She said it was because Marcus had a bruise on his neck from David leaving him in a car seat all night. Baker testified that David and Liz Carroll wrapped Marcus in a blanket and tied him up with tape and placed him in a small baby crib and put him in a closet. The small crib sat in front of the prosecutor table as he spoke. Later testimony placed the temperature that weekend at ninety degrees. The courtroom was silent; the jurors were concentrating, and most seemed disgusted.

Baker continued the story of the murder and disposal of the body.

Before leaving for the reunion Liz went back in the house from the car, and when she returned said Marcus was "freaking out." However, they left, with their dog, for the reunion anyway!

David Carroll felt uneasy about leaving Marcus the way they did; and eventually cut the weekend short to get back.

When they came back, David Carroll quickly went up the stairs to find Marcus dead. Baker said he screamed upon the discovery and Baker described David as "really scared" and "really pale." Because the kids were there, he whispered that Marcus was dead.

Liz and Amy "went up the stairs to see and he was dead. He was in the closet, in the play pen," and in the "fetal position;" Baker stated. She also testified, "there was a little blood coming from his nose and his toes kind of looked chapped like they were cracked, like the tips of his toes." According to the prosecutors, this was because Marcus rubbed his toes raw against the mesh on the playpen as he "struggled for life."

Baker continued: "I wanted to call 911. I said, let's just tell them it was an accident and he fell off the top bunk or something." I thought this interesting because this statement means that after the discovery of the body, Amy Baker was the first to suggest breaking the law by lying to the police. Baker stated, however, that both Carrolls grabbed her to prevent her from calling 911. David said rigor mortis had set in and was afraid the police would figure out how long he had been dead. As Liz sat on the floor scared, Amy said "all I can think of was to say he went missing."

The three tried to think of different stories for Marcus going missing. The first involved him getting lost among the crowd before a Bengal's game. The Bengal's game was a pre-season contest against the Washington Redskins. The date was August 13, 2005, almost ten days after the murder. I went to that game and while there, the Carroll's were up the street at Yeatmans Cove checking things out. Amy testified, however, "not enough people were on the streets at the time, and there were security cameras on corners that might have disproved such a claim." They also considered Kings Island, but again were concerned about security cameras. They decided to say he went lost in Juilfs Park in Anderson Township.

Baker testified she didn't know when Liz would go through with the story about Marcus. Liz would say she passed out and Marcus was then abducted or went missing. Coincidently, Baker said she was at the YMCA across the street from the park when Liz went through with the plan. Also at the YMCA was David Carroll. When they heard the sirens, David said "it's happening now." David Carroll then got in the pool. I thought during the testimony-- what a coincidence. Amy was just across the street from the park at the same time Liz started the plan. I was not the only one thinking this!

This action by Liz Carroll set in motion a huge volunteer effort on the part of the community to search for Marcus, the small boy with a disability. A lot of people joined the search. Liz Carroll gave a press conference at the park, calling for Marcus's return. Three people knew he was already dead.

I am sure because of his autism Marcus was a very difficult child to handle. Baker said he was "nice to everyone." "He ran up to everyone." David Carroll "would trip him when he was walking by" and give him cold baths. This part of the testimony was the saddest for me personally. I couldn't imagine a sweet and helpless child, just three years into life, being tormented like this. "He was mean to Marcus. He was really mean to Marcus," Baker stated. She also testified they sometimes bound their own kids, but only so they wouldn't think what they were doing to Marcus was wrong. They also had previously bound Marcus and "they would do it when they took their four kids to football practice."

Baker testified about the disposal of the body in great detail and it was sad testimony. David suggested the body be burned because it would eliminate the evidence. Amy suggested it be done at an old chimney near where she was raised. Marcus was eventually burned in the old chimney as Amy waited in the car. What remained of Marcus was put in a pillow case, wrapped in a trash bag and tossed over a bridge in Maysville Kentucky. A few months after this testimony, Amy Baker was indicted by a grand jury in Kentucky for abuse of a corpse, angering the prosecutor in

Clermont County because of the immunity deal he had made for her truthful testimony. This indictment was suggested by WLW radio personality Bill Cunningham who was in the audience. It was smart thinking on his part. It is amazing that no one thought of this when making the deal for immunity. Amy Baker was not served well by her attorney on this point, nor by the prosecutor who neglected to get her the Kentucky immunity. Because the citizens of Greater Cincinnati were unhappy with the plea bargain, it is with some justice that she be indicted for something related to the murder. However, I do question her being indicted for something she said under oath as part of her immunity deal.

To me the key piece of testimony was about the time Marcus was bound. In fact, for the most part, the stories of Liz and David Carroll and Amy Baker are similar. The big difference is that Amy says she didn't see Marcus bound and that Liz Carroll "said she held him and David wrapped him up." The Carroll's both say Amy helped wrap Marcus.

THE CROSS EXAMINATION

After the morning break (during the Baker testimony), Liz Carroll was brought back into the courtroom. I was able to make very brief eye contact with the accused. During that break, I asked Toni Hines what she thought of Baker's testimony so far. She said it was all lies. She said Baker was fat and a whore. Audrey Sims wandered around during the break and for a good part of it stood next to me. As her hand and mine rested on the front of the bench, they touched. It was very clear; the family of both Carroll's were angry at Baker and had immense dislike for her. The entire situation was very emotional and quite evident. The requirement for courtroom decorum is all that kept emotions in check. David Carroll's mom, small and fragile looking, seemed quiet during it all.

Greg Cohen, Carroll's attorney had said to the press leading up to today, that he couldn't wait to get Amy Baker on the stand. However, it would have to wait until after lunch. I was not about to lose my seat in the courtroom, so quickly left with the lady that was sitting next to me. We had been talking and she would attend the entire trial. We left the courthouse and headed down Main Street to a small restaurant. We each grabbed a quick sandwich and took it back to the courthouse to eat. Conversations in the restaurant were almost all about the trial and included a mix of locals and people that had come out of the courthouse. I ate my sandwich at the front of the courtroom line. In line, there was much discussion about the trial. I spoke a lot with a lady whose grandson was murdered by her daughter-in-law a few years earlier. She had his picture on the front of her t-shirt that was taken at a Reds game. After several years it was still very emotional to her. That got me thinking about one of the things I really noticed and felt about this entire day.

There was a lot of sadness in the courtroom and lives were changed the previous August that will never be the same. Being in court, you could sense the terror of Audrey Sims as her daughter faced murder charges. Debbie Hounshell was next as her son was scheduled to face the same charges next month. These two parents would forever have a loss that they will never get over. I thought of the lady from the hallway who lost a grandson---she will never completely be the same. Carrie Culbertson's mother is here at a murder trial years after the murder of her own daughter. The loss of a child no one ever loved had brought all these people together. As I well know, something will be missing from the heart of all these people the remainder of their lives. Two of them lost a child to death. Regardless of the cause they have joined the club of parents who have lost a child. It is a horrible club as I found out four years later. You are never the same. Audrey Sims has also lost her child. Audrey Sims loves her daughter as can be seen through every tear at the trial. I feel for a mother of a daughter on trial in a case like this. In some sad way it is worse than death. Her child will be alive, suffering in prison for life. A parent feels their child's pain. Audrey Sims will live her life with a pain few can imagine.

During my discussions with people from the Carroll's family, they blamed Amy Baker for everything. It was all her idea and she took the actions. They couldn't stand the fact Amy Baker had immunity. You could feel their hatred for Baker the entire time she was in the courtroom.

About 12:45 p.m., the doors to the courtroom were opened to relieve the crowded hallways. I took my same seat from the morning session. Liz Carroll entered again from the back door on the judge's right hand side. Judge Ringland entered as usual as the bailiff called "all stand." Immediately, Judge Ringland had to deal with an issue raised by defense counsel. Erin Monroe, a psychiatric nurse at Children's Hospital had left a professional journal on the table in the jury room. Presumably, she had brought the new magazine in to read during off time. One of the articles in the magazine was about autism, the same disability Marcus had. Monroe stated she had not read the article. The judge then brought in the entire jury and asked them if any read the magazine. Nobody said they had done so.

Defense Attorney Greg Cohen rose to begin cross examination of Amy Baker. After 110 minutes of suspenseful and riveting testimony, Cohen rested. His cross examination was bitterly disappointing and a terrible moment for Carroll. If she was going to be found innocent this was the time to prove it. Her goose was cooked! Cohen began by getting Baker to admit to lying to law enforcement officers in the immediate aftermath of the murder. Phil Heimlich said "I think the jury was waiting for the defense counsel to tear (her) apart." So was I. Baker admitted on the stand that she never reported the abuse of Marcus. The cross examination lasted 50 minutes and most people in the courtroom were very surprised when it ended quickly and without seemingly any impact on the case. Mike Allen said in the *Cincinnati Enquirer* that Cohen "didn't score any points." Allen is correct---Cohen had no defense. Personally, I was very unimpressed with Cohen. His slow style including speaking is not effective. He often would slowly build up to something, only to make what seemed like a minor point. He never presented any evidence of Liz Carroll's innocence.

I often watched Liz Carroll during the day and she was mostly quiet throughout. Occasionally, she would say something to Cohen and several times she would write a note. Running her hand through her long dark hair was an occasional action.

After the defense, the prosecution rose again for a few follow-up questions. In a rare move, Judge Ringland allowed the jurors to ask questions after the attorneys from both sides were finished. He would have each juror write questions on a piece of paper. If they had none, they would write that down. The Judge would then slowly read the papers and organized them in piles. Questions that could be asked were then read. They asked several of Baker.

The testimony of Baker was very interesting. This case has fascinated me from the beginning and I attended mostly because this trial would go down in Greater Cincinnati history as one of the most famous. It dominated the news and the testimony of Baker was the pinnacle of the trial.

OTHER WITNESSESS

After Baker left the witness stand, several other witnesses testified. They included:

Detective Scott Blankenship was from the Union Township Police Department. He testified about his investigation, especially what Liz Carroll and Baker bought at a Wal-Mart and a Meijer Store. What was most interesting was that the receipts he was able to obtain from the stores corroborated Bakers testimony. The times and items purchased matched perfectly and gave some credibility to her testimony.

Skip Alhorn is a chief investigator for the Hamilton County Coroner's Office. His sad testimony covered the grisly scene at the chimney where the remains of Marcus were found.

Dr. Gary Utz was the Chief Deputy of the Coroner's Office. He testified, in what to me was shocking. The bone fragments found of Marcus at the chimney would fit into a coffee cup. He showed pictures of the tiny fragments. Utz also testified that he could not determine how Marcus died. Utz impressed me with his tremendous intellect.

During Blankenship's testimony, he was prepared to show a video of David Carroll's interview from when he was arrested. However, the video equipment would not work and after about a twenty minute delay, Judge Ringland said the reason was the disc was not compatible with the court's equipment. During this time, Judge Ringland had the jury removed from the courtroom. I asked Mike Allen why he did this. Allen told me it is because the judge wanted to reduce the risk of a jury member hearing any extemporaneous statement or comment that someone might make about the trial.

During the afternoon session the cell phone of Carrie Culbertson's mother rang. The Judge glared at her for a second and then gave a very strong and angry warning.

COURT RECESSES FOR THE DAY

After the third witness, Ringland said to the court that this would be a good time to recess until tomorrow. This rare President's Day work day for the court was completed.

When the court adjourned, I immediately stood up wanting to watch Carroll leave the room and to make better eye contact. It was reported that after each day's court session, Liz Carroll would look at her Mom and say "I love you." Well, no matter what was reported, she didn't do it this time. Her Mom got out of her seat and walked toward the aisle. Remember, she was in the seat in front of me. As Audrey Sims walked just in front of me, Liz Carroll looked at me for a long time and I looked back. We made steady eye contact for about five seconds. Her mother never looked her way. In fact, Carroll looked at me longer than she did her mother. A few minutes later, I walked out the front door of the Clermont County Courthouse. Just outside the door were Audrey Sims and David Carroll's mom, Debbie Hounshell. Also with them was Toni Hines and several were smoking. I walked down the street to my car and as I drove to the corner to turn right toward home, Sims was walking down the street alone. This was an interesting sight, the woman whose daughter is on trial for murder walking a lonely path toward her car. Her daughter was back in her cell.

The next day the prosecution, and to the surprise of everyone, the defense rested after calling one insignificant witness. The following day, Liz Carroll was found guilty of murder, involuntary manslaughter, kidnapping, felonious assault, and three charges of endangering a child. Audrey Sims wailed in pain after the verdicts were read. Toni Hines and Cathy Baker tried to comfort the grief stricken mother. Later, in a hard to forget video, Sims was walking down the same street and spot where I noticed her lonely journey on Monday. She was surrounded by the media as she wailed and blamed the jury and her daughter's attorney for the verdict.

FINAL THOUGHT

The day I witnessed this famous trial was fascinating to me. As everyone who knows me understands, I love to go to historic events as they happen. This one was quite different than many of the others. It was a great experience to see but a very sad story. This trial had the murder of a child loved by no one, a murderer that was once the high school homecoming queen and class president, a husband and wife both with a female lover (Baker), a lie told to an entire community, a massive manhunt, sadness when the boy was found dead, and anger when the truth was revealed. On top of this I found Liz Carroll to be interesting in trying to understand how she so messed up her life and those of her children (biological and foster), and became a convicted murderer. To me she seemed fairly attractive and intellectual looking. Liz Carroll did not want to kill Marcus Fiesel, but she was responsible. She is a murderer. As she wept at her conviction, it was impossible to have any sympathy for her and I wondered what she must have been feeling. She was sentenced to life and is not eligible for parole for 55 years. The earliest she can be released is when she is in her eighties.

A few weeks later her husband David Carroll wisely pled guilty to avoid the same sentence as his wife. He will be eligible for parole in 15 years, although some experts say he will never be released.

There was justice this February day; however, no joy! I see evil in these two people. Seeing evil in others is not a good personality trait, but, as H.L. Mencken says, "It is a sin to believe evil of others, but it is seldom a mistake." [1]   This story is tragic and justice was served. But I guess I shouldn't call them evil. To do so makes me look elitist and righteously indigent. We are all probably no better or worse than anybody else. It's all pretense and illusion to think so. We all have our shadow to deal with, our own crosses to bear. We all have the capacity within us to be a Jesus or a Hitler.

If there is a lesson to be learned perhaps it is that Marcus was a teacher. He taught us in his short life but was not loved. No child should ever wonder what it is like to be loved.

1.   *H.L. Mencken, A Book of Burlesques, 1924*

CHAPTER EIGHTEEN
GOODBYE DELTA QUEEN

On Tuesday October 21, 2008 the Delta Queen left Cincinnati for what would be the very last time. It wasn't for sure then, but it appeared the great boat's days were numbered. Completed in 1926 for $875,000, she sailed the Sacramento River until 1940. Purchased by the Navy in 1941, she then served as a Yard Ferry Boat. After the war (1948) she was purchased by Captain Tom Greene, President of the Greene Lines of Cincinnati. Tom Greene saved the Delta Queen! After its journey to the Ohio River and renovation at Dravo, she was ready for her new life. The Greene family operated the Queen until 1974 and after Tom died, his widow, Letha, operated the company.

Current law prevents vessels with wooden super structures from having more than 50 overnight passengers on board. Since 1966, the Delta Queen had an exemption to the Safety of Lives at Sea Act. In 2008, Representative James Oberstar from Minnesota refused to allow renewal of the exemption out of the House Transportation Committee because of politics. The company that owns the Delta Queen was non-union and the Democratic Party leaders were letting union lobbyists pressure them to not renew the exemption. Thus, the Delta Queen was taken off the river. The Delta Queen had tremendous fire prevention and protection systems on board and a great safety record.

The day was beautiful and the sun was shining brightly from the west. The magnificent boat was docked at the public landing in Cincinnati. This was the last time the Delta Queen would be docked in Cincinnati. My brother, Tom, went with me and we parked in Covington at my wife's office and walked the Suspension Bridge on the east side. About 300 people attended this goodbye. From the top deck, Congressman Steve Chabot, Cincinnati Mayor Mark Mallory, and representatives of the Greene family spoke. The Congressman was optimistic that the exemption would be granted. "I look forward to seeing the Delta Queen return to Cincinnati next spring. The fight to save the Delta Queen is far from over," Chabot said. [1] Mayor Mallory gave a key to the city to the Captain, but told him he wanted it back if the exemption was granted. It would then be held to give a future captain. Tom Greene's daughter said her mother died on this boat and her father had his fatal heart attack on it. A couple small boats floated past the queen as it sat at the landing on this day. Passengers on board tied streamers to the boats side. A couple streamers fell in the river and I retrieved them for the Rabbit Hash Museum. Many people on shore had previously sailed on the Delta Queen. It would have been nice if the owners of the Queen would have let the people on the shore walk to the front of the boat, but they wouldn't.

My friend from Rabbit Hash, Don Clare, was there. Don has taken many cruises on the Delta Queen and this was a sad moment for him. Don and I wrote a book, *Along the Ohio River: Cincinnati to Louisville* in 2006. At the time Don's donkey, Higgins, was in first place for mayor of Rabbit Hash, KY. My dog, Rembrandt, was in seventh. This quirky election is actually a fundraiser for preservation of the historic river community.

 Many people on shore and on the boat held signs about saving the Delta Queen. At the end of the ceremony, the boat blew its steam whistle, providing such a beautiful sight and sound. Minutes later, the Delta Queen started to pull away from the landing. It slowly turned to go south to get fuel outside of Ludlow. As the last authentic steamboat still in operation pulled away it played the great tune "When the Saints go Marching In."

In 1811, Robert Fulton brought his steamboat, the New Orleans, through Cincinnati. This was the beginning of the Steamboat era in Cincinnati. As the Delta Queen slowly went down river, I was witnessing the end. I watched it until it approached the Suspension Bridge, transfixed by its movements and sounds. We could only hope for its revival from Congress. It never happened.

The loss of the Delta Queen and the end of the great steamboat era is described well by my friend Don Clare:

> "The day the Delta Queen left Cincinnati for the very last time was the day Cincinnati said good-bye to her long riverboat history and heritage. It was the day that

the spirits and souls of every member of the Greene family felt that awful disturbance of the spiritual world and left their peaceful resting places upon the waters of the beautiful Ohio River to the disruption and insecurity of unsettled oblivion. The City of Cincinnati was experienced at losing a significant river icon. After all, she allowed the Steamer Avalon to drift downriver to become the celebrated and last-of-a-breed authentic steam-powered packet/excursion boat, The Belle of Louisville, who will be celebrating her centennial birthday in 2014 as the oldest extant operating steam-powered river boat on our western waters inland river system. The $35,000 expenditure approved by the city fathers of Louisville proved to be the physical savior of our Ohio River history and culture. Strike One for Cincinnati!"

"Strike Two for Cincinnati turned out to be the recent abandonment of the Tall Stacks celebration in lieu of the World Choir Games. Cincinnati's culture was not defined by choirs. It was defined by steamboats and their resultant economic impact on the coffers of the city."

"Strike Three was allowing the Delta Queen to go to Chattanooga, Tennessee instead of staying in her home port and becoming the centerpiece of the Banks Project! What were you thinking, City Council? Were you thinking, City Council?"

While wrong that Cincinnati doesn't have a history of choirs, his sentiments are still potent. Cincinnati has again lost more of its heritage, never to return. The day the Delta Queen left was truly the end of the Steamboat era in Cincinnati.

1.   *Evansville Courier & Press, October 22, 2008.*

CHAPTER NINETEEN

ROBERT BYRD'S CHARLESTON FUNERAL

Senator Robert Byrd lies in state at the West Virginia Capitol

Robert Byrd was the longest serving Senator in the history of the United States. Until his death in June of 2010, he had been a United States Senator from West Virginia for every moment of my life. Byrd was one of the most interesting public figures in American history. He was an unapologetic pork barrel politician that brought billions of dollars into West Virginia. He was a student and teacher of the constitution and parliamentary procedure; in many ways a self-educated person that went to law school late in life, and an animal lover.

Byrd was elected to the United States House of Representatives in 1952 but only served six years. In 1958, the year before my birth, Byrd was elected to the United States Senate. During this time he served as Secretary of the Senate Democratic Caucus, Senate Majority Whip, Senate Majority Leader, Senate Minority Leader, President Pro tempore, Chair of the powerful Senate Appropriations Committee, and was third in line for the

presidency. [1] His record was mixed and it evolved in a manner
similar to the Country's. He filibustered the Civil Rights Act of
1964 and was a member for a time of the Ku Klux Klan. Later,
he became a spokesperson against racial intolerance. On
November 18, 2009, Byrd became the longest serving Senator in
history with 56 years and 320 days. [2] He was the last Senator to
still be serving and to have voted on Statehood for a U.S.
territory. Byrd was also a master parliamentarian and an astute
historian of the United States Senate. More than anyone, he
appreciated the history and traditions of the institution he called
home for almost sixty years.

On July 1, 2010, I drove to Charleston to watch the Byrd funeral
procession travel from the Courthouse named in his honor to the
State Capitol several miles away. I arrived in Charleston around
5:15 p.m. and parked in the mall garage behind the Robert Byrd
Federal Courthouse. Immediately I walked to the side street by
the Courthouse, past the horses that would pull the old caisson
carrying his casket. There were three white horses and one black.
The black one served as the symbolic riderless horse. Two
military transport planes flew overhead toward the airport. One
carried the body of Robert Byrd. A few minutes before the
modern black hearse arrived from the airport with Byrd's casket,
the horses were secured to the caisson. It was housed in the side
bay of the courthouse. Most people were on Virginia Street in
front of the Courthouse. I, along with about 20 other people,
were the only ones that could watch his coffin being switched
from the modern hearse to the caisson.

The side street was lined with military personnel on both sides
and a Celtic band, dressed in kilts lined up at the intersection of
Virginia Street. Byrd's caisson soon followed, pulling out of the
bay and lining up behind the band. His casket was clearly visible
through the windows of the caisson and was covered with the
West Virginia flag. A large bouquet of flowers sat on top of the
caisson as it slowly made its way onto crowded Virginia Street.
The caisson paused very briefly in front of the Robert Byrd
Federal Courthouse. I had followed the caisson and was around
fifteen feet away when it paused. People carried various signs,
including campaign signs, saying simply "Byrd West Virginia."

Behind the caisson was the riderless horse. Also following was a
large group of family, friends, and staff. Walking in the front of
the group was Governor Joe Manchin and the First Lady of West
Virginia. The slow moving caisson continued toward the capitol.

Bob with West Virginia Governor, Joe Manchin,
at the funeral of Senator Robert Byrd

Not too far up the street I jumped into the procession and many
other people did the same. As the procession made its way to the
capitol the crowd grew larger. By the time it arrived it was
certainly in the thousands. During the march to the Capitol, three
young men started to sing the John Denver song "Take Me Home
Country Roads," with the crowd joining in. Walking in the
middle of the street I did the same. All the way to the Capitol,
crowds continued to line the street. Someone gave me a small
American flag. We made our way to the back side of the Capitol
after around 40 minutes of walking. Walking in the funeral
procession felt very historic, people were both in a sad and
celebratory mood. The procession was a tremendous testimony
to the love West Virginia citizens felt toward him. It was a
powerful display. The caisson stopped at the entranceway to the
backside of the Capitol. Breaking away, I made my way to the
foot of the Capitol steps and watched as the coffin and dignitaries
made their way to the plaza halfway up the steps. A ceremony

would be taking place shortly and a color guard stood on the steps. Family and friends sat nearby.

The ceremony was brief and included a prayer and short remarks by Governor Manchin. It was really special to see the missing man formation fly above the stately grounds. Directly above our heads, one plane peeled off and flew over the Kanawha River and the nearby hill. The others flew straight. Byrd's Casket sat in front of the color guards throughout the ceremony. Lining the steps all the way up to the Capitol doors were uniformed personnel, including state police, West Virginia Guard, and Military. Also at the ceremony and standing in the front row were Senator Jay Rockefeller and his wife, and a couple former Governors including Bob Wise. When he was a Congressman, I stood next to Wise outside the U.S. Capitol during the Impeachment hearings of President Clinton and watched as he announced how he would vote on the impeachment issue.

Following the ceremony, the casket was carried up the long steps and into the Capitol. I quickly made my way over to the side of the building to get in line to enter the capitol for the public viewing. The Governor's mansion stood 100 yards behind me. The West Virginia dignitaries soon made their way out of the Capitol using the same side entrance. I said hello to Governor Manchin, shook his hand, and had my picture taken with him, as well as Senator Rockefeller. Governor Wise walked past me, although I never spoke with him. All were very complimentary of Byrd and his service to West Virginia, especially his love of his home state and as they all said he cared for the less fortunate.

It wasn't long, maybe 30 to 40 minutes, and I was in the Capitol building. Upon entering the building, there was a wreath and a picture of Byrd in front of an American flag. I was directly in front of the governor's reception room where people could leave condolences and see a few mementos of Byrd's life. As a kid I remember visiting the Capitol grounds with my father on our way to Washington D.C. I don't remember going in the building, but do remember being on the grounds and coming across a press conference held by the legendary West Virginia Governor Arch Moore. Moore served as Governor from 1969 until 1977 and from 1985-1989. He was both the 28th and 30th Governor of

West Virginia and a long term Congressman before serving as Governor. As I stood just a couple feet besides Moore, he answered reporters' questions. Years later he would plead guilty to five charges of corruption and serve time in jail.

In the Rotunda, the casket was centered on a red carpet with two State Police Officers on each side. At the precise moment I stopped in front of the casket, my cell phone rang and it was my son, Andrew. I quickly turned it off as people gave me a very, very unhappy stare. Circling the casket I headed to the reception room. As I waited in line I looked at the various items from Byrd's life including his fiddle and a copy of his album "U.S. Senator Robert Byrd: Mountain Fiddler." I signed one of the condolence books, and indicated being from Rabbit Hash, KY. Upon exiting the building, I couldn't find any transportation back to the Courthouse, and had to walk in reverse the entire route.

The thing that most impressed me about this entire event was the number of people that attended. There is no other United States Senator that would draw this size of a crowd to their funeral. He was truly loved by his West Virginia citizens and it was an historic West Virginia event. However, with Byrd the man, there is much to admire and some to question.

On one hand, he certainly took care of his state with billions of dollars of spending, was a great student of the constitution and the history and traditions of the Senate, led efforts to get cameras in the Senate, supported education, and took some tough stands when the dignity of the nation's institutions were brought into disrepute. For example, he said the impeachment charges against Clinton should be taken seriously, but did vote to dismiss the charges. He was the only Democrat to vote to censure the President. At the time I would have voted to impeach, but in hindsight I feel the proper position was censure. Byrd was right.

However, Robert Byrd was once a member of the KKK with a history of racism. Of course, he had long since disavowed these positions. In 1944, he wrote, "I shall never fight in the armed forces with a Negro by my side. Rather I should die a thousand times and see Old Glory trampled in the dirt never to rise again than to see this beloved land of ours become degraded by race

mongrel, a throwback to the blackest specimen from the wilds." [3]
In 1947 he said, "the Klan is needed today as never before, and I
am anxious to see its rebirth here in West Virginia and in every
state in the nation." [4] Almost 20 years later, he filibustered the
Civil Rights Act of 1964. In 2001, he used the term "white
niggers," in describing how race relations is talked about too
much and that "the problems are largely behind us." In
apologizing, he said "the phrase dates back to my boyhood and
has no place in today's society. In my attempt to articulate
strongly held feelings I may have offended people." [5]

Certainly an individual can reform themselves and disavow
stupid, youthful mistakes. However, joining the KKK is not a
typical youthful indiscretion. Clearly he was a white
segregationist and felt the KKK was needed, despite a history of
murder and racism. If he was a Republican, this would never
have stood. His "white niggers" statement, if made by a
Republican would have led to resignation. Senator Trent Lott
was run out of the Senate and his career ruined for saying Strom
Thurmond was right as a presidential candidate in the 1950's.
Byrd can have been a member of the KKK and it's ok? I am
completely fine with people making mistakes in speech and
apologizing. However, the double standard between Democrats
and Republicans being able to do so is very troubling. With all
that said, it is difficult to have too much respect or admiration for
a person with such overt and racist positions, even when
disavowed. However, his service does deserve respect. If you
take most of his career in the Senate it is very admirable. He is
clearly a contrast and perhaps you either love or hate him. I don't
know----he is hard to figure out!

As a side note, about 8-10 years before his death I was in the U.S.
Capitol Building on a work lobbying trip with Mayor Bill Welty
of Carrollton, KY who was the Chair of my Board of Directors.
We were in a long hallway and I said "look there is Senator Byrd,
let's go talk with him." As we approached, I said hello to the
Senator and shook his hand. I then introduced him to Bill,
saying, "this is Bill Welty, the chairperson of my Board of
Directors." Senator Byrd tersely said to me, "What did you say?"
"This is the chair of my board," was my response. The Senator

said, "No you didn't, you said chairperson. There is no such thing as chairperson, its chairman." He said something about the English language, including proper grammar, and then said, "Do you think those things out in the street are person holes, no they are manholes." After another 30 seconds of rant, we had a great discussion and he said for us to go back to his office as he was on the way to the restroom. We did so, and a few minutes later he returned. He showed us his incredible office with very, very high ceilings. From eye level up to the ceiling were pictures from throughout his career. He showed us around and described some of the framed items. One that stood out was his first ever campaign poster. He was so very gracious with his time and discussed American history, which was his passion. At the end of our time, he gave me several autographed photos. He showed his passion for traditional things, his strong combative personality, his grace and dignity, his love for history, and personal down to earth style.

As a final note, back in 1982, Byrd was facing re-election and I received a call from Congressman Clive Benedict his Senate opponent offering me a campaign job. I declined, not wanting to delay my college graduation by a semester. Byrd won with 68.49 percent of the vote. Benedict received 30.76 percent. It was a wise decision.

At the 2009 presidential inauguration, I stood outside in the bitter cold for a couple hours waiting for newly sworn-in President Barack Obama's limousine to drive by as Edward Kennedy suffered a seizure in the Capitol building across the street. It delayed President Obama's ride to the inaugural parade by at least an hour. I was soooooo frozen as was my son, Ethan. We had just witnessed the inauguration of the first African American President. Robert Byrd, sitting at the same table as Kennedy had to be taken to his office after feeling ill. Earlier in the Presidential campaign, following his victory in the West Virginia primary, Robert Byrd endorsed Barack Obama for President of the United States. Just like the nation, Robert Bryd had changed dramatically.

Byrd's health continued to decline until his death on June 27, 2010. President Obama delivered the eulogy at his funeral.

1. *Robert Bryd, Wikipedia, 2012*
2. *Robert Bryd, Wikipedia, 2012*
3. *Pianin, Eric (June 19, 2005). "A Senator's Shame: Byrd, in His New Book, Again Confronts Early Ties to KKK". The Washington Post: pp. A01. Retrieved October 3, 2006.*
4. *The Democrats' Lott", The Wall Street Journal, December 28, 2002*
5. *Top Senate Democrat apologizes for slur," CNN, March 4, 2001.*

CONCLUSION

People often ask me, "How did you get into that event?" The answer more often than not is, "I simply walked in." The average person can attend most historic events with some good planning, a little luck, and by simply going. Sometimes tickets are required, but they are usually free and often available to the public through a Congressman, Senator, or other party. Over the years, I have been fortunate to attend many of the great historical events of modern times, of which a few have been described in this book. Sure some of it may seem mundane, but I like the simple aspects of modern history; the nuances of history so often ignored. The removing of a bag on a microphone because a presidential candidate has withdrawn his concession is exciting to me. The handshake and autograph of a historic figure during an event sure to go down in history is a great piece of memorabilia. However, more than anything, what really gets me excited is the event itself. I love to read history and the question I always come back to is—What was it like to be there? This simple question guides me as an adult. I will never be known as much more than a father, husband, and simple man that lived during the end of one century and the beginning of another. That is most of our fates. However, by attending these events I feel a connection to the future long after I am gone. My future relatives can experience these events from the past because of my compulsion to journal them. Perhaps they will serve some broader historical purpose when I send them all off to the national archives someday. It makes me feel a part of events that will be known historically long after I am gone. More than anything, my journals will answer in part the question, "I wonder what it was like to be there?"

www.ingramcontent.com/pod-product-compliance
Lightning Source LLC
Chambersburg PA
CBHW032102080426

42733CB00006B/384